GETTING WHAT YOU WANT

And Being Liked For It!

How to resolve conflicts, problems, and situations with anyone about anything.

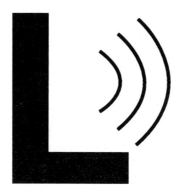

featuring the <u>proven</u> and <u>effective</u>
"Lewis Approach"
by
Charles E. Lewis, Sr. and Charles E. Lewis Jr.

GETTING WHAT YOU WANT
And Being Liked For It!
Copyright © 1998 by Charles E. Lewis, Sr. and
Charles E. Lewis Jr.
ISBN 0-9661001-0-7
All rights reserved

Printed and bound in the United States of America

Published by

Littlejohn Publishing
9903 Santa Monica Blvd., Suite 627
Beverly Hills, CA. 90212

Publisher's Cataloging-in-Publication
(Provided by Quality Books, Inc.)

Lewis, Charles Elliot, 1939-
     Getting what you want and being liked for it! : how to
resolve conflicts, problems, and situations with anyone
about anything, featuring the proven and effective L
"Lewis approach" / Charles E. Lewis, Sr. & Charles E.
Lewis, Jr. ; [editor Shyama Ross ; illustrator James E.
Lewis]. -- 1st ed.
     p. cm.
     Includes index.
     ISBN: 0-9661001-0-7
     1. Psychology, Applied. 2. Self-help techniques.   I.
Charles E. Lewis, 1965- II. Title.

BF636.L49 1998   158.2
                                  QBI98-36

This book is not intended to be a substitute for therapy or psychiatric treatment.
If professional help is needed, consult a mental health professional.

Acknowledgments

We wish to express thanks to all those individuals whose support, encouragement, and interest inspired us, as we wrote this book. They include: our family, friends, business associates, and others whose excitement about the book, and especially the questions they asked, helped motivate us to write a focused "hands-on" book that is easy to understand and to use in all situations dealing with people; especially relationships.

We specifically want to express our sincere gratitude to Mrs. Lewis and Mrs. Lewis -- our "significant others." For four years they gave us their support, encouragement, and love, as we involved ourselves in the writing of this book. Their dedication made our writing experience fun and enjoyable.

Heartfelt thanks to those individuals who shared their experiences with us throughout the years.

We wish to also thank our seasoned editor Shyama Ross, who understood our approach and inspired and helped us to make the very best presentation we could.

Thumbs up to our illustrator, James Lewis, brother of Chuck and Uncle to Charles, who drew all of the illustrations in this book. We feel his art work really helps to bring our concepts "to life."

Finally, we dedicate this book to you, the reader. We hope that you, dear reader, will also have fun and enjoyment using our approach. We especially hope that this book empowers you to handle any situation with any individual -- quickly, easily, and effectively. We hope the approach in this book helps to enrich and enhance your lives immeasurably!

Charles E. Lewis, Sr. (Chuck)

Charles E. Lewis, Jr. (Charles)

Preface

Getting what you want. Getting your needs met. Self-empowerment. Harmonious relationships. These are all objectives that all of us desire. When we get what we want, our needs are met and this gives us happiness and fulfillment. But there are things in life that we want which we cannot control; certain laws passed; ideal weather conditions on a special day; our favorite team winning the big game; our winning the lottery, etc. But there are also many things or situations which we control or significantly influence -- especially our relationships with others. Whether we want others to do or not do something for us, meet our needs, or make us happy, people do effect our emotions.

This book specifically focuses on self-empowerment: how to use words to solve your people problems, get others to do what you want, <u>and like you more for doing so!</u>

The basic concept behind our unique approach evolved over a period of over 25 years. Chuck Lewis is an expert in the field of psychology and Clinical Social Work. For years he specialized in dealing with people and families who had difficult and complicated emotional problems. Through his work -- and successes -- he created this new, fresh, and pointedly different approach. He was able to draw on his experiences in dealing with thousands of people throughout the years in his profession as a Licensed Clinical Social Worker. Eventually, he modified his approach to handle virtually all everyday, practical situations that normal people experience. Soon, his wife and only son, Charles Jr., and other close family members began to use parts of the Lewis Approach with exceptional and satisfying results.

In late 1992, Charles Jr. experienced a confrontational verbal situation at work. Upon Chuck's recommendation, Charles began to use parts of the approach in this book to solve his problem. The results amazed Charles. His situation at work was resolved quickly thanks to using the approach. Chuck had helped other close family members through similar situations for years, as well as Charles. One evening, Chuck and Charles got together in an aura of excitement. They knew the time had come to document this approach. They wanted others to benefit using the approach the way they had. Thus, the bare beginnings of a book had begun. Finally, in early 1994, Charles decided to "take the bull by the horns" and arranged for this book to be written. After he organized notes, records, past situations, etc., the two began writing. Over the four years it took to write this book, Chuck and Charles focused like a laser beam on the concepts and approach so that they would work every time for anyone and be effective in solving the common everyday problems that we all have. They devoted many hours to make sure the presentation was easy for people to understand and to use. Charles created and developed important concepts used in this book. In fact, before the book was completely finished, Chuck had considered Charles to be a master of the approach.

As they wrote the book, Chuck and Charles worked with people who wanted to <u>start</u> using the approach to solve their people problems. The results people had were astounding. In fact, everyone who has worked with Chuck and Charles, using just one or two of the many principles of the approach, has found it easy to do and tremendously effective. The most often-heard comment was how very different their approach was from anything they had heard of or read before -- and how easy to understand and to do. People immediately wanted copies of this book before we had even finished three quarters of it! This delightful and very positive response helped to inspire us, the authors. It also bolstered our motivation to finish this book. We wanted to help as many others as we could to solve their problems with people. We wanted them to get what they wanted from others more often, more harmoniously, and to enjoy their lives more.

This book is not a therapy book filled with abstract theories or complex phrases which require a doctorate degree to understand. This book is a vital and real life hands-on book! If offers specific phrases and words you can say to help you easily solve problems with people. Chuck and Charles share personal experiences with you that focus with crystal clarity on helping <u>you get the results you want</u>.

We know there are many useful self help books and resources available that may help you. We feel strongly, though, that our book differs from others. We go beyond where most other books leave off! Not only do we teach you the concepts and approach so that you understand "what" and "why," we also explicitly show you "how." We give detailed examples, written in dialogue format, that offer actual scenarios in common situations, which you can use. Further, we show how the other person will react and what they will say <u>before</u> they even say it. Essentially, we combine a "one of a kind" approach you will not find anywhere else -- (i.e. specific things to say to solve your people problems speedily and effectively). This gives you the skills you have been searching for in vain in other books and sources.

Over the past two decades, Chuck has developed and used this approach effectively in a large variety of situations; with family members, friends, neighbors, couples, parents, children, employers/employees -- just about everybody. More recently, Charles has successfully used the approach at home, work, with friends, with family, and in other situations. Both Chuck and Charles have begun to teach this approach to a few select close friends and family members. They have received much positive feedback and heard many success stories from these individuals. After reading this book, Chuck and Charles are confident that in a very short time you will also be able to use their approach as easily as they do and achieve the same type of positive results. As a result, your life -- and those of others -- will be greatly enriched.

Table of Contents

Introduction

Throughout the years, we have all heard phrases such as: "You must love yourself before you can love others.". "If you work hard and play by the rules, you'll get all you want.". "Apply yourself and focus on being number one.". "Get that house or new car you want." These are all desirable objectives. But no one seems to be able to tell us exactly HOW to achieve these goals. No one offers a solution that is practical, understandable, and applicable to our particular situation. No one offers a solution that _will actually work virtually all the time in any situation_!

What should we do ? We simply adapt ourselves to our environment and cope as best we can. We try to be nice and pleasant and avoid painful or frustrating confrontations. But one day our frustrations reach their peak. We get fed up, explode, and express our true feelings. Now, we have an "enemy" who is angry at us -- and we have still not gotten what we wanted!

In this book, you will learn how to get what you want by using "positive selfishness" -- which means loving yourself as you are. You will learn how to use a concept called "direct anger" - which is a healthy use of anger without creating enemies. The practical dynamics which result from using our basic approach is that others do the work freely -- and love doing so! Moreover, others will instinctively like you more!

The "Lewis Approach" is not designed to manipulate, force, or coerce others into doing things that they don't want to do. It is designed to help us do three important things: a. to decide what we want, b. how to skillfully tell others how to give us what we want, c. how to make it easy for them to do just that!

If you want to manipulate others to make them do things, our approach will not work for you. (It may work once in a while but not with any consistency; and in the long run may backfire.) Conversely, using our approach works consistently and to everyone's ultimate satisfaction.

<u>What This Book Is</u>

This book is a practical, how-to-book for people who want results easily, quickly and pleasantly. It is <u>not</u> a therapy book; It is not designed to get you to *change* yourself or anyone else. Rather, it guides you to <u>*focus on getting what you want*</u>, but not at the other person's expense.

This book provides you with a clear and specific way to instruct and guide people to respond to _your_ needs and wants and to increase your happiness as well as those of others. Both parties will get what they want and feel good about it! The simplicity of the "Lewis Approach" at first makes it difficult for people to believe it is strong enough to work. But, in fact, it is actually _more powerful_ and _more effective_ than any usual or conventional approaches.

The basic approach of this book is, quite simply, revolutionary. Essentially, it is comparable to finding a cure for the common cold. This book actually gives you a "magic pill" in respect to dealing with people, personally and professionally. In situations where you have felt uneasy, uncomfortable, even angry, haven't you wished for some "magic words" to erase the unpleasant experience and the accompanying unpleasant emotion?

This book offers you the approach that does just that except that this is not magic. It is real; a unique approach that works! The "Lewis Approach!"

There may be other concepts, theories, or techniques which you have heard of or used before that seem similar to the "Lewis Approach." But they are not. In fact, over 25 years of developing and using our approach in private practice, clients who have used our unique methods quickly see the distinct difference. They experience success that they never had before or even dreamed possible. Clients report greater happiness with the results they get.

As you begin to use the "Lewis Approach," we are confident that each of you will also report similar success that others have found. What distinguishes our approach from all others is that we do not make or force people to do things, we show people how to please us and themselves simultaneously -- and love every moment of it. No one is forced, manipulated, or coerced. The decision to have others please us and give us what we want is their own free choice. We show you how to take responsibility for telling others how to please us and help them succeed in this to everyone's satisfaction!

By using our simple and powerful approach, you become in control of yourself, your situation, and your life. And others freely and happily respond to your needs without sacrificing their own. You get what you most want, plus you please yourself and the other person in any situation anytime!

Chapter 1

See Yourself as Perfect the Way You Are

How can you most effectively get what you want...and be more liked for it? To begin with, think of yourself as being perfect the way you are. You may not always be correct but you are perfect. This is very important. Why? It means that all of the good about you is perfect, all of the bad about you is perfect, the mistakes you make are perfect, etc. In short, you are perfect simply by being *you*.

If you see yourself from this perspective, you can then focus your attention on what others are telling you. This is crucial. It helps you to better decide what their words mean to you. Then you would know what to do. You would know how best to react, instead of being defensive or rejecting of what is said to you - whether it is "good" or "bad". This implies that everything about yourself is perfect _for you_. You may not be seen as perfect by other people, but you are perfect to yourself. Conversely, you must also view other people being as perfect for who they are - good, bad, or indifferent.

Why is this so important? If you see yourself as bad or imperfect, you then see yourself as "wrong" and become unhappy with yourself. No one likes to be wrong. To see yourself as perfect prevents you from judging yourself or feeling defensive. Then you can focus on the issue itself rather than try to figure out who was right and who was wrong. In other words, seeing yourself a perfect as you are precludes being defensive. It lets you really hear what the other person is saying. If you don't see yourself as perfect, you will inevitably become defensive and not listen to what issue or issues are being raised. This will create problems in your dialog. Others will feel they have to work harder to prove their point or get their message across. These types of ordinary conversational processes almost always lead to an argument or disagreement, often needlessly.

But when you see yourself as perfect, you prevent this from happening, provide a better avenue to hear the issues, and reach satisfactory solutions. Even if you've made a mistake or have done wrong, when you see yourself as perfect, you allow the person to help you correct the problem. You change your "perfect wrong" to a "perfect right;" and the other person helps you do this and feels much better.

However, if you do not see yourself as perfect the way you are, the other person may try to manipulate you. How? Firstly, by making you feel guilty, which exerts unnecessary pressure on you. Most importantly, you may be locked into a mind set which resists change, attack the other person, or try to explain the reason for your behavior. This leaves you open to being judged or reprimanded for doing wrong. This inevitably leads to conflict and unhappiness.

Furthermore, if you don't see yourself as perfect, your self-esteem is lowered, which can zap your energy and drive. Then you begin to feel depressed. In effect, you are turning the anger, frustration, and bad feelings in on yourself. Then you try to change what you don't like about yourself and try to correct your mistakes. But when you view yourself as perfect as you are, you can focus on your needs as opposed to trying to change yourself. This is a positive use of energy.

The point to remember is: when _you_ are ready to make a change, you will do so! You cannot change before you are ready. For example. if you regard some behavior of yours as bad and try to change yourself, the other person will try to change you the way _they_ think you should be changed. This makes you defensive. Moreover, this process could continue indefinitely and ultimately irritate you. Again, see yourself as perfect, then _focus on getting your needs met_!

To illustrate: say you have a fear of heights and your friends invite you to join them on the top of a very tall building to view the city. If you refuse, they might call you "chicken." This is a form of manipulation. To handle this, you could say, "Let me be chicken." This statement has a dual effect. Firstly, you are telling the person _what to do_ to make you happy: to let you be. Secondly, it implies that you are perfect the way you are. If you are chicken, you are a perfect one! This prevents you from being manipulated and puts you in _control_ of what _you_ want. Further, you are instructing others on what to do to please you. Thus, you avoid becoming defensive. You stay focused on what _you_ want. If they challenge, saying: "You always spoil the fun.," you still stay focused on what you want. You might respond: "Let me spoil it. Go ahead and let me wait for you here." You are focused and clear on what _you_ want. "Let me spoil it." implies that you are perfect the way you are. This is a simple example of getting what you want!

Conversely, if you see the other person as being bad or having flaws, you will try to change them and create a problem. See others as perfect as well as yourself. In fact, see yourself surrounded by perfect people. We are all perfect people living in an imperfect world. Worldly imperfections create problems between people and cause them to do things they might not otherwise do. Does this mean you have to like or accept people's choices or behavior? No. It simply prevents you from judging, evaluating, or condemning others. Moreover, it enables you to focus on helping that perfect person please _you_ or make _you_ happy.

Your focus is always on getting *your* needs met rather than proving others right or wrong, etc.

Always Perfect But Not Infallible

Some people have told us they find it hard to think this way because they make mistakes. We all make mistakes. We've all heard the phrase, "Nobody is perfect." Even when you make a mistake, you must see yourself and your mistake as perfect. Perfect, but not necessarily correct. Mistakes arise from pressures, stressful experiences, or specific circumstances. Circumstances are not perfect, but you are. For your own emotional health and well being, you must correct your mistakes.

Let's take this point another step further. Let's say that you arrive at ten a.m. for a 9:30 a.m. meeting. Is that being perfect? Yes! You arrived to the meeting late perfectly. And you will deal with amending or rectifying your lateness perfectly as well. But your perfection at *being you* is intact.

Why is this concept so important? Despite your behavior, the mind set to see yourself as perfect precludes feeling guilty. It frees you to assume responsibility for you actions, eliminates the need to become defensive, or to justify what you have done. Whatever you have done, you have done being perfect as you are.

Assuming this mindset of being perfect as you are also helps the other person to be more clear about their problem with your behavior. It allows them to focus on the problem instead of trying to verbally attack you or explain why you were wrong.

Double Benefit

Thus, the value of seeing yourself as perfect the way you are has a double benefit: It prevents you from being manipulated, forced, coerced, or persuaded by others. It also helps them deal with you in a positive and constructive manner, and to stay focused on your issue or what you want. If someone is negative or judgmental toward you, it won't be an issue if you see yourself as perfect the way you are. You now have a solid platform on which to work from to help others satisfy your needs and please you as well as themselves. Essentially, this mindset protects you from being susceptible to adverse statements, feeling judged, or from becoming defensive. Seeing yourself and others as perfect gives you the _power_ to stay focused. Specific ways to do this are discussed in great detail in the Chapter entitled Anger.

Chapter 2

Positive Selfishness = Loving Yourself

What is Positive Selfishness?

One of the first things to do to achieve your objective is to be selfish in a <u>positive</u> way; Love yourself! Positive selfishness and loving yourself are the same. Loving yourself is basically a state of mind. Using our process of positive selfishness tells you <u>how</u> to love yourself. The primary focus in positive selfishness is to think only of your needs and having those needs met. Do not consider the needs of the other person. That is his or her responsibility. Your first reaction might be that this is difficult to do and that people will have a hard time with your doing this. But they don't. Over the years we, and those we have helped, have each used positive selfishness in many different situations. In every instance, the other person never noticed our approach or felt slighted. Keep in mind, however, that being selfish in a positive way _does not mean you force others to do anything._ Rather, you _educate_ them so that they _want_ to help you. That is truly being loving: when people do things for you because they _want_ to. You do not force, convince, coerce, or trick anyone into doing anything. (In the long run, these always backfire.) When people do things for you because they _want_ to, you feel more comfortable receiving and they feel comfortable giving! This is a result of loving yourself - i.e. positive selfishness.

Remember, there is a positive and negative way of being selfish. The negative way is to have your needs met at the _expense_ of other people. This creates competition. We feel we must win, that we must _beat_ the other person in order to get our needs met. We think we must prevent others from getting what they want in order to get what we want.

Positive selfishness (the positive way of being selfish) means we get what we want at no one's expense. The "Lewis Approach" yields a win-win situation for both parties. We focus on _our_ needs and work toward that goal. We always stay focused on what we want. If the other person is also selfish in a positive way, you have a very positive and constructive communication.

For example, let's say your friend George wants to see a film and you want to go the ball game. If you say, "George, you always want to see films.," that is a put-down of him. If his response is: "You never do what I want to do.," that is a put-down of you. This creates an argument. To avoid this, stay focused on going to the ball game, but don't prevent George from wanting to see the film. This will help him to go along with you. Your role is help George <u>understand</u> how to do what <u>you</u> want done and its importance to you. As an automatic part of this process, George, without putting you down, will be able to focus on how important going to see a film is to <u>him</u>. The result? Both you and George will know what would work best for the two of you and be able to make a decision that is mutually satisfying. A win-win situation.

We are all born selfish. From childhood on, the id (the desire for self pleasure) dictates our actions. This is most noticeable in young children. Later on, parents and schooling teach children social skills: learning to share, courtesy, consideration, respect, and so forth. These social interaction skills are learned skills. The basic drive in human nature remains selfish, the desire for self pleasure.

Unfortunately, learning these social interaction skills often confuse us about what actually constitutes selfishness. We interpret social skills to mean to be unselfish. Thus, children learn at an early age to keep "selfish" feelings to themselves. They are taught to think of the feelings of others. The result? Children have difficulty in distinguishing "being selfish" from using social skills. Gradually, a child becomes increasingly dependent on feedback from others to determine whether they are doing what is socially acceptable or not. Thus, a child compromises his or her own feelings and begins to think more and more of others. The reality is that one can be successful by being both selfish and possessing excellent social skills. The two are not incompatible. In fact, the two are a healthy combination.

As we become adults, we think of the needs of others as well as our own. We try to analyze the needs and wants of others. We decide how best to interact with others and still get what we want. This approach is inevitably frustrating. How can we figure out what others want since they often do not clearly know what they want? Each of us has a hard enough time trying to clarify our own needs.

If neither person asserts positive selfishness, and helps the other person understand how to give them what they want, they both experience more anxiety, tension, or frustration. Using positive selfishness to help people please you and do what *you* want them to do, does *not* preclude having effective social skills. In fact, it improves your social skills! Applying positive selfishness makes it easier for people to understand *your* point of view. If a person clearly understands your point of view they are in a better position to make you happy.

We have been taught by our parents, educators, and others to think of other people first, to share, and to be friendly with our neighbors. This is designed to teach skills in interacting with others. Basically, this is sound teaching - overall a good way to think and to behave. The emphasis in this philosophy was on promoting social skills, rather than on denouncing selfishness. When you use positive selfishness, you are being social in a positive way. You are creating a healthy climate to help people please you and share in your happiness. This concept, positive selfishness, actually gives others the power to please!

Why You Use Positive Selfishness

When we use positive selfishness, we clarify and direct others on how we want things done. People are more inclined to do things for you when you use positive selfishness. The better they understand what it is that you want, the easier for them to comply. Sometimes it is hard for people to truly be selfish in a positive way. Why? Because you have to first know _exactly_ what you want. You learn this by focusing first and foremost on yourself. This is an example of loving yourself in a positive. You cannot depend on others to know what you want. We all have a tendency to depend on others to help us know our needs. The reality is that it is next to impossible for someone else to truly know what _you_ want. When we depend on others to know what we want, it becomes a "hit-or-miss" proposition for the other person. Even if the other person is able to figure out what we want, they will usually give us what we want _their way_, rather than _our way_. This can create a problem. When they give you what you want _their_ way, you may not recognize that you got what you wanted! This may sound strange, but it is true.

Positive Selfishness Enhances Social Interaction

What constitutes effective social interaction? When both people involved derive pleasure from the interchange. If people are truly using positive selfishness, they would get their needs met most of the time. When you are with friends, and you feel things are going well, to your satisfaction, you feel good. Obviously, the more we get what we want, the better we feel. And if your friends get their needs met as well, everyone is satisfied and has a good time.

Mutual positive selfishness results in mutual satisfaction. So being selfish, in a positive way, can and does improve social interaction. It places the responsibility of getting your needs met on _you_ instead of other people. You are in control. A healthy person is a responsible person.

Only _you_ really know what your needs are and if they are being met. No one else can know this. This also reduces the chances of your becoming frustrated. It allows you to control how your needs get met. When you leave the responsibility for getting your needs met to others, you become dependent. In any dependent position, you inevitably experience more anxiety because you don't know what to really expect. This decreases your chances of getting what you want. The other person, unsure of what you really want, may be hesitant to act. Thus, he or she would be unable to effectively meet your needs. Then you feel angry and frustrated when your needs are not satisfied.

If you are not selfish in a positive way, you may soon become selfish in a _negative_ way - usually at someone else's expense. You might eventually accuse others of not doing things for you, despite the fact you never explicitly told them _what_ to do for you, what _your_ specific needs are.

For example, you might tell a friend, "Why do you always bring your friend with you? All he does is drink and carry on. He's un-classy. Why can't you come by yourself?" This is being selfish in a negative way. What do you really want? You want your friend to come alone or without this particular friend. Instead of saying so directly, you criticize him in the hope that he will "get the message."

Using positive selfishness in this same situation, tell your friend, "When you come over, come by yourself and let's spend time together. I'd really appreciate that." This is being selfish in a positive way. You are focused on telling your friend _what_ to do for you and _how_ to do it, without criticizing him. Using positive selfishness is much more successful, more open, and allows you to interact in a much more productive way.

Another example involves a couple in a counseling session about to have a confrontation. We stopped them and said, "Try being selfish to get what you want." They began to focus on their needs instead of trying to get the other person to change. The result? The problem immediately began to resolve itself.

The fact that the husband and wife became more selfish and tried to get their own needs met helped them gain clarity as to what they wanted; it also showed each other how to achieve mutual satisfaction. Both people gained control of the situation. The other person could decide if they wanted to please the other person and, in the process, also please themselves. Thus, they could both be pleased with the outcome.

Using positive selfishness produces positive results. It gives both parties the power to please themselves (i.e. get their needs met) while, simultaneously, pleasing the other. When others please you, they feel better about themselves and your needs are met!

How You Use Positive Selfishness

What being selfish in a positive way accomplishes: 1. You identify things that you want that will make you happy. 2. You tell people how to give you those things. 3. You focus on getting your needs met. In effect, you are loving yourself in a healthy way. There is one very important qualifier you must keep in mind. Never be selfish at someone else's expense. That is not positive selfishness. In order to use positive selfishness as defined in this book, it must meet two criteria.

Firstly, what you want must come only from you - not be tied to what someone else wants. It must be only from you and only for you. An example would be to want something solely because someone else wants it. Secondly, it must <u>not</u> be done at another's expense. The other person must always have the freedom to choose between doing or not doing what you want them to do. These two criteria constitute positive selfishness.

We have experienced in our lives that when people use positive selfishness, (i.e. focus on their needs and tell people how to please them, but allow others freedom of choice), they almost always get what they want. And in cases where they didn't, it was <u>beyond the person's ability to please</u>, even though they wanted to do so.

Getting your needs met, without forcing people to do what you want them to do, is also being positive socially. You clarify what you want, but accept their decision to please you or not. However, if a person does not please you, it does not necessarily mean that they don't like you or are angry with you. It may mean: a) they can't do it (i.e. lack the ability); b) they do not know how to do it; c) it is not important enough to them. As we continue to help the person to please us, we try to determine if it is a, b, or c, that is preventing them from pleasing us. Then, we are better able help them make the decision to please us. If they do not know <u>how</u> to do it, we teach them how. If it is not important enough for them, you would help them see the importance to <u>you</u>. When they decide to please you, they are really making a choice to please themselves! They feel successful. They are pleasing themselves at no cost to you. That is being selfish in a healthy way. This is a very important point in understanding positive selfishness.

The following is an example of how the use of positive selfishness works when dealing with a person on something you want.

A person wanted to change an appointment with his friend. He said: "I need to have you change your appointment to six o'clock because I have another commitment." The friend replied, "I can't do that because I need to take my aunt home." Obviously, we have a conflict here. The person tried to make this appointment time important to his friend. He said," This is really important. We need to get together at six o'clock." He used an analogy. If your mother had to have surgery, would you tell her you could not come because you had to take your aunt home or would you would find a way to rearrange your schedule? This six o'clock appointment change is that important to me, so work out a way and get back to me." The friend became defensive and said: "I really need to take my aunt home at that time. She is on medication and needs to take it at certain times. Thus far, nothing has been resolved and they both feel guilty. If the person had been selfish and thought exclusively of his own needs, he would have told the friend only how to do, leaving the decision to the other person. Thus, his friend would have felt less defensive.

Here's how using positive selfishness would have worked. The person could say: "Let's change the appointment time from three o'clock to six o'clock, that would be better for me." The friend would not feel criticized nor rejected. The friend may have replied: "I can't do that because I need to take my aunt home at that time."

The person responds: "I understand, but this is important to me so work something out so we can meet at six o'clock." The words "I understand" are important words to use. It lets the other person know that you recognize what they are saying is important to them. Using the phrase, "so work something out..." begins the process of helping the friend understand how important it is that the appointment be changed.

This phrase uses Direct Anger to help the friend please him. Whenever you express anger, you will automatically feel a sense of guilt. To reduce these automatic feelings of guilt, the person should add: "I would appreciate that." The statement: "I really need to take my aunt home at this time; she is on medication and needs to take it at certain times." reveals the obstacles he faces in changing the time. The friend is being selfish by sticking to his original plan: taking his aunt home by six o'clock. Even though each person is being selfish, no one is being verbally attacked or getting hurt. This is using positive selfishness.

If the friend says, "I understand how important it is that you take your aunt home at six o'clock, but, it's still important to me that you make this change. Arrange to take her home earlier so we can meet at six o'clock." The friend now sees the importance this has to the person. They would then clarify the importance of their own situation. One of them would then make a decision to please the other, which would also please the decision maker. Please note that neither one "gives in" or "compromises." Rather, the decision maker makes a decision to please himself. This is a very important point. If the friend decided to meet at six o'clock, the person would reward the friend for the decision. The person might say: "I'm glad you were able to work that out," or "Thanks for arranging that for me." The friend would feel good about his decision and take this comment as approval and acceptance. This is one simple example of how you can have people please you by using positive selfishness.

One more significant point relates to positive selfishness. As much as you are able, avoid bringing a negative to yourself. That is, don't point out your own negatives. Leave that to others. If you point out your own negatives, especially if you do so frequently, people will have a tendency to use those against you. For example, if someone criticizes you for doing something wrong, don't respond with, "Why are you saying that I'm not doing it correctly?" or, "Well, I do tend to be sloppy." These statements pass judgment on yourself and give the impression that you intended to do it incorrectly or sloppily. Instead say: *"Tell me why you think it is not correct"*. Notice we left the "I" out and said "it" instead. This keeps you from passing judgment on yourself or feeling defensive. You will also be more open to hear what the person is saying and be able to better make a decision to act, or not act, on what the person is telling you.

How Positive Selfishness Eliminates Conflicts

Being selfish in a healthy and positive way reduces conflicts with other people. Being selfish focuses only on your needs and what you want the other person to do for you. Why is it important to think only of your needs rather than what the other person wants? Because the message you convey comes strictly from you and what you want, instead of mixing in what you *think* the other person wants or wants to hear. That only confuses the situation. If you are not selfish, and you include things you believe the other person wants, this makes it more difficult for the other person to understand what *you* really want. They may thus fail to do what you want, because you gave them incorrect information. The bottom line is that your lack of being selfish prevented them from clearly understanding what you wanted, making it more difficult for them to please you. When you are selfish, you convey clarity as to what you want, making it easier for others to please you better. When you focus only on getting your needs met, don't confront others. Without confrontation, people respond positively and don't feel criticized. Criticism invariably feels like rejection. When people are confronted, or feel rejected, they will usually fight back, become defensive, and not really listen to you. They then create a host of reasons to avoid doing what you want them to do to please you. This will happen when they are not opposed to what you want them to do! People only object to your being selfish or getting what you want if it interferes with their own wants, or prevents them from being selfish in a positive way.

Selfishness decreases conflicts. The more selfish you become (telling others what to do for you and how to give you that), the more others become selfish and tell you how to meet their needs. This eliminates dependency on both sides. Each one takes more responsibility for getting respective needs met! This process reduces conflict, confusion, and frustration, and always increases clarity. There are no hidden agendas, no manipulations, and no "figuring out" what others want. Further, it eliminates the desire to be defensive or to justify yourself. You stay focused solely on using positive selfishness to help the person to please you. This greatly improves the chances for both parties to get their needs met. Obviously, when people get their needs met, they feel good. That's why this concept of positive selfishness has worked so well over the years for the authors and those they have worked with, in both personal and professional situations.

Chapter 3

Anger

What is Anger?

For the purpose of this book and the tools and steps we offer, anger is defined simply as "change" agent. Most of us _perceive_ the expression of anger as being critical, throwing a tantrum, or being out of control. But in truth, anger is the only "change" agent we have to move us toward happiness.

For example, let's say you're at home watching television and you feel hungry. What motivates you leave your comfortable position on the couch and get food? Anger. The physical sensation of an empty growling stomach creates a need. In this case, for food. In order to satisfy your need, sufficient anger had to build up to motivate you to satisfy that need. Thus, anger served as a change agent to satisfy you. Without this change agent, nothing would change.

Anger, as a change agent, arises from frustration, disappointment, irritation, anxiety, or any emotion that causes us to feel discomfort. In effect, anger results from anything that prevents you from getting what you want. When you experience any unpleasant emotion, your needs are not being met, your happiness is being interrupted, or your progress is being blocked. Anger arises when your brain signals to you that you are <u>not</u> getting what you want. Anger fuels the energy to get those needs met.

Like most of us, you may be angry without even knowing it. How to recognize when you are angry? This is <u>important</u>. If you don't even know you are angry, you can't effectively use the steps to get what you want. Again, the primary source of anger is generated from needs not being met: Situations where you want something to happen and it doesn't; when something happens that you don't want to happen; or when someone imposes their value system on you. In these situations, we are bound to feel either disappointed and upset, which could quickly lead to anger. Any situation or experience where our needs are either thwarted or unfilled awaken anger within us.

In any situation where you are being judged by another person's value system, you may try to explain yourself. But what you are actually doing is criticizing the other person. When you try to explain yourself, <u>it is as if</u>

you are saying to the other person, "Let me explain this to you because you are stupid." Obviously, this is a criticism. More importantly, what you are doing is trying to change the other person's thinking. However, once you explain your position, the other person will explain his or her position. Your reaction? The same as theirs: You'd feel criticized. The reaction may be either conscious or subconscious.

This above type of projected dialog could go on indefinitely, and eventually evolve into an argument. Neither person is happy with the other and, in fact, both of you would feel uncomfortable. This is a very common basis for most arguments. In such a projected dialog exchange, you may be unaware of your anger. The anger, however, works beneath the surface. Whenever you feel defensive and compelled to explain your position to someone, you are angry - whether you are able to acknowledge this or not.

From another perspective, when you are in a discussion with another person, and they appear frustrated and begin to explain their position to you, strongly consider the possibility of <u>your</u> being angry. Why? You may be putting "road blocks" in the other person's way as they attempt to make their point with you. This may be a conscious or unconscious act.

The bottom line is, we all want to be understood. When we feel we are not understood, we get angry. It's that simple. Although the degrees of anger may vary from person to person. In our communication with others, we are focused on having the other person understand our position and, to a lesser degree, understanding the other person's position. That is the basic nature of communication. When we feel misunderstood, it naturally follows that we try harder to make our point. All of this effort can quickly lead to frustration and then anger. Learn to recognize your growing anger in such situations. This is vital for you. You can then properly utilize the "Lewis Approach" to be effective in getting what you want. In situations where you feel frustrated, uncomfortable, anxious, or uneasy, recognize this as your being angry!

To illustrate: If you are engaged in conversation with someone, and you begin to feel other than "normal," (i.e. uneasy, irritated, anxious, excited, defensive, uncomfortable, etc.) recognize these as symptoms of anger. But let us point out here, this is a _healthy_ anger. If you are not feeling "okay," you are angry in a healthy way. Accept this fact without denying it or becoming defensive. Even though you may not _feel_ angry, you are and need to recognize that. When you accept that you are angry, you can then use that energy to correct how you feel. _You can use healthy anger in a positive way._

Use Healthy Anger Positively

Clearly instruct the person to listen to your point. This focuses the conversation to your point of view and helps the person meet your need to be heard and acknowledged. Otherwise, you'll become defensive; this creates a "road block" to the person listening to you, causing them to be defensive as well.

To illustrate how this works: You and your business partner are discussing office locations. Your partner says: "You always pick the wrong places. You'd be out of your mind to locate there." Your response might be: "Listen to what I have to say, ask me questions about it, and tell me what you understand." Here you are effective in clearly instructing the person to listen to your point and respond in a way that you'd like. This helps the person to hear and be more open to your point. If you responded with a criticism or an attack, you'd put "road blocks" in the person's way and they close off listening to you at all.

Another aspect to emphasize: Most people do not like getting angry and will resist it. Instead, they will demonstrate what we call "denial." Sometimes, this denial is verbal. A classic example is when a person tells you, "Don't get upset." And you reply, "I'm not upset!" This statement denies your true feeling. Although you sound upset and may even appear upset, you may not even feel upset, due to your denial. Why the denial? Usually, to avoid dealing with a particular issue. You choose to "deny" the anger because you don't know how to deal with a particular problem. Another reason is you may not want to experience the passive anger that many people utilize in trying to solve their problems. You may also feel you might lose control of your anger and say or do things you would later regret. Thus, the alternative many people chose is to simply avoid and/or "deny" anger.

It is crucial to recognize the possibility of being in "denial." Then, you will be better able to determine *if* you are angry and, if you are, you'd be in a better position to deal with those feelings accordingly. Avoid denying your feelings of healthy anger and accept the possibility that you may be angry.

Once you have the *tools* to deal with any problem you are facing, "denial" will not be a viable option. When you learn to utilize the steps ("tools") that we have detailed in this book, you will effectively be able to deal with the problems and situations that life presents to you. You will then transfer healthy anger into positive ways.

<u>Passive and Direct Anger</u>

Basically, there are overall two types of anger, Passive and Direct. There are others ways to view anger, but these two types clarify the explanations and make them easier to recognize. You will be able to successfully utilize the "Lewis Approach" when you view anger from these two perspectives.

<u>Passive Anger</u>

Passive anger, also known as indirect anger, is a very dependent and weak position. Passive anger is basically non-communication. You expect something from others without verbalizing clearly what you want or need. This anger is also a "change" agent: It tries to change your situation or position from one thing to another. You may expect someone to do something for you without even knowing yourself what you want. Obviously, you cannot reasonably expect anyone to figure out what to do for you when you yourself cannot articulate clearly your needs. Only by luck or coincidence someone may fulfill your expectations.

Mostly, it is difficult, if not impossible, to have someone magically meet your needs without _you_ telling them what to do for you! When you create such expectations for yourself, and the person does not come through for you, you feel hurt and disappointed. Since you felt dependent on that person to please you, and they didn't, you become angry, which could lead to an unpleasant conversation.

How is passive anger expressed? Typically, when people are critical, complain, shout, act sarcastic, blame, manipulate, coerce, question, accuse, become verbally abusive, or exhibit negative behavior. Why are these traits labeled passive? The user of passive anger does not take responsibility for getting his needs met. The effect of passive anger is to cause hurt, confusion, or pain - which makes it very difficult to communicate. This is why most of us don't know how to communicate successfully. We all have a tendency to avoid telling people how we really feel. So out of fear we resort to using passive anger when we address issues with people. We then fall into the trap of judging and criticizing the other person, but we never tell them what to do for us or how to please us. We would rather not tell them that part. Why? To do so would be direct anger, which we will discuss in detail later on.

Why do people even use passive anger? Because we are all born in a state of dependency and we resist the idea <u>taking responsibility for getting our needs met</u>. It is easier to blame others for not meeting our needs than for us to accept our failure in getting our own needs by communicating them to others. Virtually, everyone communicates in this way. We know from experience that every argument is based on passive anger. In fact, you cannot have an argument without passive anger being used!

This seems ironic in light of the fact that both the person expressing and the person receiving passive anger feel "bad," (i.e. uncomfortable, even pained). Why? The one expressing passive anger is usually unhappy about a situation. They are not getting what they want and feel frustrated or anxious. The one receiving the passive anger is being criticized for letting the other person down. This person is then pressured to explain or defend their behavior. But the needs are still not met. Why? Because the receiver is unclear about what the person wants, usually because the person expressing passive anger is unable to articulate his or her needs.

An example of how passive anger is revealed in conversation:

Larry failed to come to his friend Joan's party.

Dialog.

Joan: "Why didn't you come to my party?"
Larry: "I was busy."
Joan: "Why are you always busy when I want you to do something for me?"
Larry: "I'm not always busy. I spend a lot of time with you."
Joan: "You are never too busy for your friends. Why do you always have time for them?"
Larry: "You know, you always nag me. Do you treat your friends like that?"

Sounds like a typical conversation, doesn't it? This dialog can go on for minutes, hours, days, or longer. As a matter of fact, some people develop patterns of communicating this way <u>all the time</u>. But such unproductive dialog creates negative and stressful relations with people. It is obvious that neither Joan nor Larry are happy with each other. But it is not even clear exactly what Joan wanted. Yes, she did ask him why he did not come to her party. But, did she simply want to know his reason or was she trying to convey her anger that he didn't show up? Did she, in fact, have other "issues" with him? (i.e., he is always late or never comes to events, etc.) Using passive anger, Joan was not taking responsibility for getting her needs met. She never effectively communicated them. She simply asked questions. She never specifically told him what she wanted him to do to please her. The argument was caused directly by <u>passive anger</u> being used.

This type of use of passive anger is expressed by <u>most</u> people most of the time. Why? Because they think it works for them. They believe they are standing up for themselves. People believe that when they express passive anger they are more powerful. They are used to expressing their feelings in such an indirect way. They seem to get a bigger reaction. So, they continue to do so, despite the uncomfortable feelings they experience. Is there a better way? Definitely!

When you want to get your needs met, <u>avoid using passive anger</u>. It's a dead end. Too many negative things happen to you. Again, passive anger is a painful anger for both parties involved.

How To Detect Uses of Passive Anger

How can you tell when someone is using passive anger? They use the following words to start their sentences: Why?, Could?, How come?, Why don't?, You should..., You shouldn't..., You always..., etc.

Passive anger is not totally bad per se. We all express passive anger at times. It simply reveals that we feel insecure about a situation or event and use it as a defense, though weak. Being able to recognize passive anger will help you understand the situation and help you to act accordingly, using the steps taught in this book. Remember, when a person asks questions, especially several in a row, they are usually expressing passive anger. (See Questions).

Passive anger is used when a person is dependent or in a dependent role or position. Dependency is counting on the other person to know what we want, and to satisfy our needs, without our telling them! When you don't get what you want (and chances are you won't), you feel disappointed and become angry. Alternatively, the person may do what you wanted them to do, but it may not be the <u>way</u> you wanted it. So, you would still be upset. For example, a woman may want her boyfriend to buy her a gift for her birthday and tell him this. But, he may buy what she does not feel is appropriate - such as, a box of chocolates when she is on a diet and trying to lose weight.

<u>Being dependent on others to get our needs met, and using passive means to get those needs met, is the biggest cause of problems between people.</u>

<u>Direct Anger</u>

Direct anger is healthy anger. Essentially it is the main tool to get what you want. It is *absolutely essential* for success in using the "Lewis Approach." In direct anger you take responsibility to communicate to another exactly what your needs are, how they can be met, and instruct the person to do that for you. You assume full responsibility for getting your needs met. Direct anger gives clear and concise instructions on how to please you.

Using direct anger, you utilize <u>*action*</u> words which instruct people how to please you, emphasizing the importance the issue has to you. This taps into the innate desire in human nature to _want_ to please others. People like pleasing others. We all do. You also directly instruct people what to do _for you_ to meet your needs and make you happy. You do not depend on the other person to "figure out" what you want, even if you think they should know this. Your responsibility is to help people to meet your needs.

By utilizing direct anger, you _empower_ the person to have the knowledge, ability, and motivation to please you. Direct anger is also a change agent; it creates the change that _you_ want - (i.e., getting your needs met. Your situation or position changes from one state of mind to another. Direct anger allows you to effectively resolve any differences _much faster_ because it focuses the problem- solving process on the issue (i.e. what _you_ want) and helps things to progress more smoothly and positively.

When you use direct anger, think only of your needs and not the needs of others. This may sound strange, but people like and respect you for thinking only of your needs. Why? Because you are clear and explicit as to what _you_ want. This gives others a sense of importance in your life. It also conveys your confidence in them. These make people feel good. They may not be consciously aware of this, but we know from experience that this is precisely how people respond.

When you use direct anger, don't try to force the other person to do anything. This is an infringement on a person's "free will" - their ability to do what they want and their freedom to choose. People like pleasing others. But if they sense you are trying to force them, they will subconsciously feel as if their free will, or power to choose, to please you or not, is being violated. When people sense this (even if your motive is unintentional), they will resist.

Using Direct Anger

How then do you use direct anger? Begin your sentences with an *action* verb. Use actions words (verbs) that direct, clarify, and instruct. Start sentences with words such as: Go, Do, Give, Take, Tell, Handle, Remove, Explain, Describe, Let, Allow, Say, Be, etc. The following are examples of phrases to illustrate:

- o "Tell me if you can get here by three o'clock."
- o "Go to the store for me."
- o "Give me time to think about that."

These words make it easier for the other person to do what you want them to do for you. They also give the person the _option_ to exercise their free will. Give them clear and concise guidelines on how to please you and what would make you happy. Implicit in all this: You are telling the other person how to be successful with you.

Direct Anger = Loving Yourself

One of the most important points about direct anger is: It is loving to the person expressing and to the person receiving. You express *love to yourself* when you focus on getting your own needs met and communicating what makes you happy. And it expresses love for the person receiving because it _empowers_ them to be a success with you. You are telling them what to do _for you_ to make you happy; and when they feel that they made you happy, they feel pleased. When we get our needs met, we essentially feel loved.

For example, you may ask a guest to spend more time with you. But they may have another engagement. Your responsibility is to tell the person the importance their staying has to you: "I know you have to go, but stay a little while longer. _It is important to me. I'd appreciate it._"

At this point, both of you will most likely have a clear picture of what would make each of you happy. The person might respond: "I'll stay five more minutes and then leave." You might reply, "Okay. Let's arrange for you to stay longer next time. Tell me if that works for you."

Analyzing this dialog, it is clear that neither side is being criticized. Both have given instructions and information about themselves. Both conveyed clear guidelines as to what will please them. Each person has taken responsibility for their needs being met.

Sometimes, of course, you may use our approach this way and people may not do what you want them to do for you _right away_. This will not happen very often, however, if you use our approach correctly. If this does happen, keep in mind that this is normal. Some people respond more quickly, or more slowly, than others. In any event, keep using direct anger, using the action verbs and words, as outlined. People will come around eventually and please you: When they resolve their own concerns about what you want and decide that _what you want them to do for you is more important to you than what they want_.

An example of how this would work. If your lover/mate planned to attend the theater, but you wanted them to stay home. An effective way to deal with this without a big hassle, problems, or arguments, would be for you to say: "Change your mind about going to the theater tonight and stay here with me. I'd feel better about that." If the person challenges you, your response could be: "I understand what you are saying. But, change that for me. Make me happy and work it out to stay here with me anyway. I'd really appreciate that." (See "Getting What You Want - Comprehensive Examples.)

When you begin to use direct anger, as taught in this book, you may at first feel strange or uneasy. This is normal. This feeling of anxiety will diminish as you continue to use the direct anger and see the positive results. Focus on using direct anger to guide others to do what you want them to do for you. The reason for initial anxiety is because you feel the weight of your own responsibility for getting your needs met even though you are directing the other person to do things to please you. Positive Selfishness is a new experience for many of us. The success of the outcome is now squarely on you. Anxiety results from the shift of a dependent role (expecting people to know what you want without telling them) to taking an independent role (taking the responsibility of directing the person to please you).

Another reason for anxiety: You may feel the statements or instructions you give to the person to please you (i.e. direct anger) may not feel powerful enough. You may also resist the idea of taking full responsibility in directing the other person to meet your needs. It may feel safer to remain being dependent on them to meet your needs and not use direct anger. But use direct anger because these feelings of anxiety and resistance will pass. Keep using the direct anger! This is the best approach to help the person to make you happy or please you. Remember, the only change agent you have is anger, which no one likes to express.

As the person begins to go along with you, especially when you are helping another person overcome resistance, keep using direct anger. Resist the tendency to stop and depend on the other person to know what to do for you. Be persistent in using the healthy and positive method of direct anger. *You must continue to express direct anger to get what you want.*

Bear in mind, when you are using direct anger, neither you nor the other person will feel as if you are using anger at all! This is one of the most intriguing characteristics about using the "Lewis Approach." For the first time, you will be able to use the most powerful and direct forms of anger, and not even feel anger! Many years ago, a very successful martial arts specialist described his fighting style as the art of fighting _without_ fighting. _How_ he did his martial arts may have _looked_ like fighting, but his extreme success and effectiveness was based on art, control, and other features. In terms of this book, think of direct anger _as "The Art Of Using Anger Without Being Angry"._

Remember, using direct anger precludes yelling, criticizing, being sarcastic, manipulative, or anything negative or destructive! You only use direct anger to instruct people to please you and make you happy. Using this direct anger is using the most powerful and positive form of anger one can use! Why? Because you are aware of what you want, take control of what you want, and then guide the other person to give you what you want!

Direct Anger = A Healthy Power

Most importantly, perhaps, the other person will not mind you using this with them. Direct anger is the anger that "does not come back at you." When you use direct anger with people, they will not see it as anger at all. They will see it as your liking and caring about them. In so doing, you don't get any passive or negative anger back from the person. Rather, people feel better with you and want to please. In fact, when you use it, the person will like you even more. The controls are in your hands to guide people to get your needs met. This may not sound all that powerful; punching someone may sound more powerful. However, by the time you finish reading this book and have implemented these steps yourself, we are confident

51

that you will experience directly the power of direct anger and reap the positive rewards.

As we have said before, when most people think of using a powerful anger, they think of yelling, screaming, making threats, bulging their eyes, and, perhaps, even resorting to violence. All of these "powerful acts" are, in reality, very weak! <u>They are very weak and dependent positions</u>, relying on some one else's actions, not their own. For example, if a person said, "If you don't give me the money, I'm going to punch you." Who is really in control? The one with the money or the potential puncher? The one who has the money! He can decide to either give the money or not. The "puncher" cannot do anything until the "money holder" acts. Thus the "money holder" has control. On the surface, it may appear like the "puncher" has power. He doesn't. Further, if the "puncher" actually punched someone, they still have no control. The person with the money will have gotten punched, but would still dictate and control what happens with the money. Additionally, the "puncher" would <u>automatically feel some guilt</u> - either immediately or later. The "puncher" would feel this guilt because he knows that physically hurting someone is wrong. The "puncher" often denies feelings of guilt and tries to suppress them, asserting that the person who got punched deserved it. However, this does not eliminate the feelings of guilt, it only attempts to justify the guilt! The fact remains that the guilt still exists. Using direct anger always puts you in control of your life space, in a healthy and non-combative way!

Direct Anger is Pleasure Based

When you use direct anger, you do not feel the anger because the focus is to get *your* needs met rather than judging or trying to change the other. (You will "feel" anger only when you express passive anger.) Direct anger is considered "pleasure based" because *you take charge of your life space.* You guide the person and constantly give them directions to do what *you* want them to do *for you.* The anger that exists is a "focused anger." You do not control the person, but you actively influence their input or entry into your life space. You always remain focused on your needs rather than dealing with the other person's needs.

When others decide to make you happy and please you, reward them with words of praise:

o "I appreciate what you did."
o "Thank you. It means a lot to me."
o "I'm happy you did that for me."

These statements also help relieve any guilt you may feel as a result of using direct anger. Be aware that any time you express anger (any kind of anger), there will be guilt.

Let's explore the term "pleasure based" in relation to direct anger. Why is direct anger "pleasure based?" It pleases both the person expressing and the person receiving. When you use direct anger, you do not receive opposition. The person with whom you are using the direct anger is given information as to how to please you, and they have the freedom to respond accordingly. Most importantly, if they do what you want them to do, they are guaranteed to be successful with you and receive rewards. This is the crucial reason why direct anger is not felt, (i.e., you do not feel the anger). It is reward/success based, rather than criticism based. It short, it is pleasure based. How can you feel you are expressing anger when the results are so positive? Usually, we associate anger with bad feelings. But, when you use direct anger, you do not <u>feel</u> the anger. You feel good.

Now you are responsible for directing the other person to be a success with you as well. Take control of directing the person to please you. However, never try to control someone. As stated earlier, if people even think that you are trying to control them, they will resist and may even verbally attack you. People resent this, so don't try to control the other person. Focus only on giving the person direction to meet your needs. This is the only type of control that you need to deal with: Giving clear direction.

When using the "Lewis Approach," it is your responsibility to clearly help the other person meet your needs. Be aware of any internal anxiety within you. But as you continue to use direct anger to help the person meet your needs, your feelings of anxiety will slowly evaporate.

There may be a temptation to assume that the person will figure out the rest of what you want them to do after he or she begins to go along with you. Resist this. Continue to use your direct anger to instruct them fully and clearly through the completion about what you want them to do. This is an <u>important</u> part of the process. To assume the person can figure out what you want them to do for you would be a step back into a dependent state, where the chances of getting your needs met would decrease.

The following is an example of how our approach is used when dealing with an aggressive or violent person. Notice how we kept focused only on getting what <u>we</u> wanted, yet we did nothing to stop the other person from trying to get what he wanted. We both had an equal right to get what we each wanted. Notice the other person's reaction and especially the words we've underlined. These are action words, what we call direct anger. These verbs are <u>absolutely essential in using the "Lewis Approach."</u>

George is yelling and screaming and making accusations. Here's the conversation.

We: "George, <u>lower</u> your voice."
George: "I don't want to lower my voice because I'm upset."
We: "I understand that but <u>lower</u> your voice anyway, I would appreciate that."
George: (His voice lowered). "No one thinks about me or what I want."
We:" <u>Sit</u> down and <u>talk</u> to me. <u>Tell</u> me what upset you.
George: (His voice raises again). "Why do I have to sit down? No one else has to sit down."
We: "<u>Lower</u> your voice for me, George. I would appreciate that."

George: (His voice lowers again). "I didn't mean to raise my voice again."
We: "That makes me feel better. Thanks. Tell me what upsets you."

By using these direct anger words, we gave George **structure**. In his attempt to please us (by his response to the direct action words used) he was then able to be more successful with us. But he also pleased himself because it was his free choice to comply. This decision was based on his pleasing himself as well. He wanted to be successful with us. As we focused on positive selfishness and on our needs, George began to be more selfish and think only of his needs. Eventually, George began to automatically use the same type of action words we had used. Our approach actually helped him as well as us.

On the other hand, if we had tried to prevent George from raising his voice, (i.e. "If you don't lower your voice, you'll have to leave."), he would have seen this as rejection, and the situation would have escalated and gotten out of hand. No one likes to be ordered or forced to change when they have no choice in the matter. If George began to tell us what to do, we would not have liked that either and would have felt upset.

The distinguishing characteristic of our approach is, we tell people how to please us. We **do not order** them. We do not try to force or coerce them to do anything. We honor their free will and leave the decision to please us (or not) up to them. We respect their choice. However, it's your responsibility to tell people how to please you and to help them be successful doing that. Again, we all like to please others. Even our enemies like to please us. It is important to internalize this fact. It is one of the most important points in our book. Inevitably, when you tell people how to please you, they may not automatically do so. Why? There may be a number of reasons for this. These will be explored in the section, "Getting Through Resistance".

Before we move on to the next section, here is a detailed example of the power and effectiveness of Using Direct Anger. Firstly, however, we will show how people use passive anger - typically what people who are in a dependent position use.

A couple, John and Mary, had recently split up. John had Mary's CD player and Mary wanted it back. Here's their conversation:

Mary: "I want my CD player back."
John: "I'm not going to give you your CD player back until you give me my picture back."
Mary: "What picture?"
John: "The one that I gave you two Christmas' ago."
Mary: "That's my picture. You gave it to me."
John: "Well, I had to give you your TV back. What about that?"
Mary: "I only loaned that to you. I didn't give that to you."

Based on this dialog, do you think Mary will get her CD player back? We don't think so. At this point, Mary felt she needed to take a stronger position:

Mary: "If you don't give me my CD player back, I will sue you."

Do you think this will work? John's response? He decided he'd take a stronger position:

John: "Oh yeah? Well I'll sue you too, for the cost of my fixing your car."

These two statements of John and Mary may sound forceful or powerful to you. The fact is, they are very weak. No one is getting anything and there is no resolution in sight. If they were to actually act on their threats, each of them would expend much energy, time, and money - and they'd still be very upset with each other!

What is happening here? No one is taking **responsibility** for getting their needs met! Both John and Mary are totally depending on the other person to meet their needs. This situation could have been successfully resolved if one of them became more selfish about their needs and used direct anger to get those needs met.

To illustrate the power and effectiveness of Using Direct Anger, here is the conversation using direct anger.

Mary: "John, give me my CD player back."

John: "I'm not going to give you your CD player back until you give me my picture back."

Mary: "I understand that you want your picture back and we'll talk about that in a minute. In the meantime, arrange to return my CD player back this weekend when I am home."

John: "Well, will I get my picture back?"

Mary: "I can understand what you are saying. But, let's talk about your returning my CD player. Arrange to bring it back on Saturday. I would appreciate that."

John: "You're gonna have to sue me first!"

Mary: "No, don't tell me to sue you. Make it easy for me and bring my CD player back this Saturday. I would like that."

John: "Why should I bring it back to you?"

Mary: "John, go out of your way for me. It is important for me to get my CD player back. Do this for me."

John: "Well, what are you gonna to do for me? You always want me to do things for you. What will you do for me."

Mary: "Don't ask me to do anything for you. Make me happy and bring back my CD player this Saturday. I'd really like that."

Do you think John is now more likely to return Mary's CD player in this situation? We think so. Personally, we have had this situation happen many times. In every instance, each person got what he or she wanted. Even if John did not return the CD player, both of them would feel a lot better as a result of this dialog. Most likely if this type of conversation continued over a period of time, John would eventually return the CD player. When John did return the CD player, Mary would then thank him for doing so. She could tell him how happy it made her or how this pleased her. We must always **reward** people for pleasing us. When you acknowledge that you got what you wanted, you don't feel guilty. Again, another healthy result of the use of direct anger.

Anger is Like "Emotional" Money

Anger is like "emotional" money. When you feel frustrated, anxious, fearful, worried, disappointed, etc., view these feelings of anger as money. Why? All of these feelings represent your needs not being met; your not getting what you want. Use your anger (direct), as you would use money: to get what you want.

We use money to buy what we want: food, clothing, candy, movies tickets, etc. If we have the money, we can buy whatever we want. In short, we can get what we want with the use of money. But, when you use passive anger (become upset, shout, blame others, etc.) you will not get anything for your "money." View this type of anger ("emotional" money) like counterfeit money; people will not honor it. Instead, they will resist or fight you. Replace using that type of "money" (passive anger) and get something for your "money" by using direct anger. Direct anger is like using real "money." You use this "money" (direct anger) to tell people how to do things for you and give you want you want. People will honor this "money."

Remember, the main reason for anger: we are not getting our needs met. Our progress is being blocked, either physically, emotionally, or spiritually. Our anger serves to give us the energy to get our needs met or to remove barriers that impede our progress.

When we view anger from the perspective of "money," we begin to see how our anger can be used to our advantage - to get what we want. Then we can focus our anger effectively.

For example, Philip bought a sports car and showed his girlfriend Alice.

Alice: "Does it seat children?"
Philip: "You are so stupid! Of course not. What happened to your common sense?"
Alice: "You are the one that's stupid. Why are you buying a car like that? You can't even afford it."
Philip: "How do you know what I can afford? You can't do anything right yourself; you can't keep a job, you can't keep a clean house. How do you think you can take care of your children if you can barely take care of yourself?"
Alice: "You are the one who lost your job. You're such an idiot. You spend you life savings on a car when you don't even have a job."

In this example, each person is using anger (money) passively and getting "nothing for their money."

How could Alice use anger like money? After Philip's verbal abuse,

Alice: "Stop talking to me like that and be nicer to me."
Philip: "I'm not going to be nice to you. You are not nice to me."
Alice: "Philip, be nice to me and say things good about me. I'd like that."
Philip: "Why should I?"
Alice: "I understand that. Just be nice to me. I'd appreciate that."

In this instance, Alice is using her anger like money (direct anger) to get what she wanted: for Philip to be nicer to her. In doing so, she focused on telling him _how_ to talk to her in a way that _she_ liked. Use your anger like money to instruct people what to do for you or how to give you what you want.

Let's consider a situation where you use anger (money) but do <u>not</u> get anything in return. In this case, your money (anger) is being wasted. For example, if a friend criticized you for eating junk food and you felt upset and became angry, you could use this anger as money.

You might respond: "You always criticize me about the food I eat."
Your friend: "You told me you wanted a better diet."
You: "Well, that was yesterday."
Your Friend: "You always change your mind. I never know what you want."

You: "If you were really concerned about me, you would know."

Obviously, here the anger (money) is *not* being used to get what you want. The conversation is going nowhere, nor does it sound friendly or beneficial to anyone. Your friend does not seem to be getting what she wants either. Both are expending lots of anger (money) and getting nothing. No matter how much anger you expend here, you are not getting what you want. This type of fruitless interaction occurs frequently with people. Then they wonder why they are not satisfied.

Let's discuss the flip-side of this example. Your friend tells you that you are eating junk food. As soon as you feel the anger build inside you *think of your anger as being money.* Your next thought is, what do you want to get for your money (anger): To *tell the other person to do something for you.* This is an important point to emphasize. To do this, you have to figure out what *you* want. Do you really want your friend to refrain from criticizing the food you eat and let you enjoy it? You could tell your friend to join you in eating. Or, you could tell them to discuss the topic of food and diet next week. The important thing is: to get what you want from the other person with your real money (direct anger) by telling them to do something for you! You don't use it to throw your counterfeit money (passive anger) all over the place with insults and judgments of the other person and wind up with nothing but hostility coming back at you.

Sometimes we think we may get what we want by criticizing others. This doesn't works. Criticism only stirs resentment. It's like "burning a bridge" with another person. You figure if the other person won't give you what you want, you might as might as well get the satisfaction of insulting or criticizing that person. However, this may sound justified, but it is not. Why? You now have made the person angry with you, and they may verbally attack you. Further, when you criticize someone, you automatically experience natural feelings of guilt. Anytime you criticize someone, even if they deserve it, you will have some sense of guilt.

It is important to emphasize here that if you do not use the anger to get what you want, the anger will build up inside of you and cause you to feel bad or depressed. Direct anger is a *positive* tool to help you get what you want. Moreover, it fuels you with the necessary energy to <u>get your needs met</u>. If you do not use this healthy anger to get your needs met, you remain unsatisfied and frustrated, which further increases the anger within you. Then depression sets in. Avoid these unpleasant and negative feelings and use the real money (direct anger) to get what you want. You'll please yourself as others please themselves simultaneously. It really works!

How To Use One Anger At A Time: Direct Anger

Virtually everyone dislikes expressing anger. We try to avoid it. We try to be nice, passive, pleasant, easygoing, etc. But when we are forced to express anger, due mainly to our level of insecurity, we often express more anger than necessary. We go overboard and use two or more angers simultaneously. When using our approach and when under pressure, use only **one** anger at a time. Use only direct anger. This shows independence, which is all that you need. The second anger, and all subsequent "angers" used at one time, represents a person's need to feel <u>dependent</u> on others. We have a tendency to start piling on the "angers" - believing that more angers are more effective. Thus, we may mix passive anger with direct anger and speak with intensity and increased loudness, rage, etc. No matter how expressive or volatile, these other angers are passive and show dependency. We add them because we feel anxious or insecure about using anger and being dependent on others. To avoid anxiety, insecurity, and being dependent, use one anger at a time. **Use the positive and healthy anger: direct anger.**

Using other angers is really an attempt to force others to do your will and rob them of their own free choice. Remember: you can never happily get your needs met at the expense of another person. If you attempt to control others, they will resist. As stated before, no one likes to be controlled, forced, intimidated, or bullied into doing anything.

Direct anger is a loving anger, it gives clear instructions as to how to please you and make you happy. If you mix other angers in with direct anger, it negates the effect of the direct anger.

Example: "Go get my coat from the cleaners, which you should have done earlier." Go is a direct anger word; should implies criticism and is passive anger. Though the direct anger is there, the receiver never hears it because it has been negated by the passive anger, which may include a criticizing and aggressive tone of voice.

Insecurity and strong dependence are almost always the *root* of passive anger. It is a desperate attempt to get your needs met. Note that the word "should" is a judgmental term, which can automatically put a person on the defensive. It implies that a person is doing something wrong or not doing something that they ought to. When you use such words, you are not taking responsibility for getting your needs met. Only the use of direct anger alone can convey that message.

Questions are also passive anger and must not be mixed with direct anger. Implied in any question can be a criticism or a judgment. For example, "Why couldn't you remember?" or "Why do you always forget?" This insults one's intelligence.

Let us emphasize again that when you mix direct anger with other "angers," such as passive anger or harsh or abrupt voice tones, people will react to the "second" or other anger. They will not hear your use of direct anger. The person will be more focused on resisting what you want them to do. This means more work for you and the increased possibility that they may not do at all what you want. Therefore, use only one direct anger at a time.

Summary: the use of only direct anger results in positive reactions. It feels better for both you and the other person. More importantly, you will be much more effective with people. Best of all, perhaps, people will begin to do more things for you and like doing so! Direct anger results in successful communication. Successful communication results in successful and happy relationships!

Instructions (Direct Anger) & Questions (Passive Anger)

Instructions (Direct Anger)

Using instructions when dealing with people is a healthy way to communicate. Instructions do not judge, criticize, demand, intimidate, threaten, or create any negativity. What they do is give effective guidelines for the other person to follow. Most importantly of all, it **empowers** them to take action for you. From another perspective, using instructions with others means you are in **control** of your own life space; and it also means directing people into that space so they can be more successful with you. This process automatically raises your self esteem, your feelings of self worth, and reduces your need to be dependent on others. Please note that instructions we discuss in this section, and throughout this book, are Direct Anger.

For the purposes of this book, Instructions and Direct Anger are the same. Instructions as discussed here help to illustrate the form Direct Anger takes in practice. It starts with the use of an *action* word (a verb) in telling (instructing) the person what to do for you. It takes direct responsibility for getting your needs met.

Let us illustrate with a story: You are feeling insecure on a day when a very important person is due to visit you. You want to make a positive impression on that person who is a "chain smoker." You have a dilemma: You do not want anyone to smoke in your house. What can you do? Use instructions (direct anger) with the person! Example: You: "I know you smoke so I have arranged a place for you to smoke on the porch. When you want to smoke, use the porch. I'd appreciate that." The instruction statement is "smoke there" (the porch). An effective use of direct anger. Emphasize the importance this issue has to you: "I'd appreciate that." Using instructions in this way makes your message very hard to resist.

What if this important person resists: "I don't want to go outside to smoke. I'll be spending more time outside than inside." Let the person know that you heard them, then continue to use instructions: "I'm glad you've told me this. I wasn't aware you felt that way. *But make this easy for me and do it the way I want you to do it; smoke on the porch instead of in the house.* I'd really appreciate that." These instructions do not criticize, intimidate, or demand. They simply give good guidelines for the person to follow and further *empowers* them to take action for you. Note the initial phrase: "I'm glad you've told me this. I wasn't aware you felt that way." This is using our concept of "Positive Acknowledgment" (discussed in another chapter). It shows _acceptance_ of the other person - which reduces their desire to resist you. It places the person in a better position to be more receptive and please you.

Using instructions such as this is most effective when you anticipate the other person's opposition. Using instructions helps to reduce resistance and guides others to focus on your issue. This is important because if you reduce the resistance, you have more energy to focus on obtaining your desired results. But if you spend much time fighting off resistance, you may soon end up feeling frustrated and give up. This could cause you to be angry for the rest of the day, and beyond. Anticipate resistance when you focus on getting what you want. Use instruction statements frequently to diffuse this.

Another point: Instructions may be improperly used from a negative standpoint. In the above example, we didn't tell the smoker what not to do. We didn't use negative words. This is important and done by design. It is an integral part of our approach. Using our approach, avoid using negative words such as: couldn't, shouldn't, won't, can't, etc. Replace these words with positive instructional statements that tells others what to do for you (rather than what not to do). For example, if you wanted someone to do something for you and they resisted and asked many questions, you'd respond: "Ask me those questions later." Don't say: "You _shouldn't_ ask so many questions." Another positive response: "I know you have questions, but let me get back to those."

Honor Others

Negative words block other people's progress and causes them to feel angry and, to some extent, eager to battle with you. You block their progress when you tell them <u>not</u> to do something for you. Be positive: Focus on giving people instructions as to what to <u>do</u> for you. This makes things much easier for both of you and makes you happy.

As stated previously, in using instructions (direct anger), don't think that you have to bully people around and tell them to do all kinds of things. People resent that and will resist. However, do instruct people and tell them to do things *for you*. This may sound like a mixed message. To clarify, if you use harsh language and try to bully people around to do things which seem to have no specific meaning or purpose and without telling them what to do <u>for you</u>, people will not follow your instructions. Further, if you use instructions but omit telling the person the *importance* the issue has to you, people will again tend to resist and question you. To avoid these undesirable results, frequently use instructions to provide a clear message as to what and/or how you want the person to do something *for you*. As often as possible, emphasizing the high level of importance the issue has to you. Using instructions in this way makes it much easier for people to follow your instructions and be happy doing things *for you*. The focus always remains on using instructions to help people <u>do things for</u> <u>you</u>, but not to try to change them. You use instructions when you want people to do things in your life space, rather than theirs.

Instructional Statements give clear, concise, and directional messages to others regarding your needs. Additionally, they convey a sense of **mastery** and **confidence** in what you are doing. People become more cooperative because they instinctively believe that you are in command of yourself. And, in fact, course, you are! You are giving the person instructions as to what to do to make you happy.

However, this is not one-sided. The other person benefits as well. What you expect of them becomes clear and easier for them to do. Most importantly, since it is not a put-down, the other person has no need to become defensive. This leaves them free to focus their attention on how they can do what you want them to do rather than expending energy defending themselves or verbally attacking you. Using instructions (Direct Anger) makes it easier to keep yourself and the other person focused on your important issue: Getting What You Want.

Summary: using instructions, when dealing with people, is a **healthy** way of communicating. Instructions (direct anger) do not criticize, threaten, intimidate, or do anything negative. They give good guidelines for the other person to follow and **empowers** them to take action for you.

Questions (Passive Anger)

Questions are virtually the opposite of giving instructions. Questions, as defined throughout this book, are a form of Passive Anger. From our perspective, Questions and Passive Anger are the same. There are, however, other forms of Passive Anger, such as yelling, being sarcastic, manipulating, etc. Why is asking questions Passive Anger? Because questions <u>do not</u> take responsibility for getting your needs met. They leave that up to the other person.

Questions are an expression of passive anger; which are painful to the person expressing it and to the person receiving it. Avoid this kind of anger. If you ask a person many questions and do so indefinitely, the person begins to feel irritated with your questioning, and a negative conversation may ensue. For example, if you ask a person three straight questions, after the third question, you will very likely get an irritable response from that person, no matter how simple the questions are.

A simple illustration. Question #1: "How are you doing today?" The person responds, "Fine". So far so good. Question #2: "Did you sleep well last night?" The response, "Yeah". Question #3: "Did you have breakfast yet?" At this point the person may react negatively, either verbally or by body language. Or, their attention may focus more intently on you as they try to ascertain your motives. If you continued to ask questions regardless of this reaction, the other person would soon begin to ask aggressive or confrontational type questions in response to yours. For instance: "Why do you want to know so much?" or "How come you are asking so many questions?"

Questions are also designed to extract information from the other person. For example, questions about where a person was born, where they lived, where they went to high school, etc. You would also be controlling the person's responses because these questions are restrictive in terms of how you can answer. The question, "Where were you born?" could not receive the answer, "I had eggs for breakfast." That would not make sense. Your question restricts the person to a specific answer.

Many Questions = Controlling Others

Why is this issue about questions significant? When you ask questions, you are attempting to control the person to whom you are talking. Since that person does not know where these questions are leading, there is an element of uncertainty and the unknown. Remember, people tend to resist uncertainty or the unknown, which generally creates scary or uneasy feelings that most people seek to avoid. To take this point one step further: Have you ever noticed how most people dislike being a witness in a courtroom? Do you know why? A main reason is that people fear being manipulated into saying things they may not mean. Another reason is that people have no control in a courtroom situation. They must answer the questions the attorney asks. They are controlled by the questions and, under the laws of the court, witnesses must only answer the questions asked. Witnesses do not have the freedom to elaborate.

Let us further explore the courtroom scenario. When you look at the issue of questions in a courtroom, the questions do manipulate the witness to give answers closer to the response the attorney wants in order to win his or her case. Courtroom questions are highly manipulative. In a court of law, an adversarial relationship exists. One side is fighting the other. Both defense attorney's and prosecuting attorney's want to manipulate the witness to emphasize their own point of view. The method used is "questioning." We don't know anybody who <u>likes</u> being a witness in a court of law.

As discussed in the chapter on Anger, questions are passive aggression (i.e. indirect anger) which is painful to express and painful to receive. Obviously, courtroom type excessive questioning would be a decided turn off when dealing with friends, family, acquaintances, or business associates.

Naturally, most of us do ask people questions in order to manipulate others into making statements which support our own viewpoint. Then, we use their answers against them. For example:

A wife asks her husband: "Didn't you know I had to work late today?"
The husband replies: "Yes."

Wife: "And didn't I tell you that I would not be able to cook today?"

Husband: "Yes."

Wife: "Didn't I also hear you tell me that you had the day off from work today?"

Husband: "Yes."

Wife (exclaims): "Then why didn't you get dinner for us?"

Husband: "Well, you didn't ask me to."

Wife: "Well, get a clue. You should have known. What happened to your common sense?"

Husband: "You are such a nag. Why are you like that?"

As is apparent, in all of those questions, the wife set up the husband to prove her point and strengthen her argument. After the husband answered all of those questions, many of the explanations that he could have used were eliminated, based on the way he answered. Thus, the husband was effectively controlled and manipulated into responding to the questions in the way his wife wanted him to respond. Notice how they are in a very uncomfortable discussion. If this conversation were to continue, the husband would start to ask more questions as well, thus perpetuating the conflict. Both would have been culpable in contributing to this argumentative situation.

How To Respond To Questions

Then, how do you respond to questions? What is the healthy and effective way to respond to a barrage of questions? To avoid being controlled, manipulated, create an argument, or have a negative experience: Stop answering and asking questions - after the third one is answered. This eliminates the problem of the unknown. More importantly, it allows you to get a bearing as to where you are headed. Instead, instruct the person to tell you what information they want. After the third question, state clearly: "I want to give the correct information so tell (use of direct anger) me what you want to know." If the person is trying to control your responses, they may not stop asking you questions so easily. They may continue to ask questions, such as, "Why won't you answer me?" Don't answer that question! Instead, respond: "That's a good question." Then, restate your statement, "Tell me what you want to know." Repeat this statement two more times, if necessary. By then, the person will respond and tell you what they want. Thus, you will have avoided a negative conversation.

Challenging Questions

In situations where people who are upset with you ask questions, they are really not interested in the answers. You may think they are and they may think so too. But they are not. Challenging questions are:

a. "Why didn't you go to the store like you promised?"
b. "How come you didn't call me?"
c. "Where were you this afternoon?"

These all reveal an angry or upset state of mind. Do you think the person will be satisfied if you respond to these apparently straightforward questions? Would the person be satisfied if you respond: "I was busy," or "I forgot," or "I was going to do that later?" No, they wouldn't. In fact, they'd probably view these answers as excuses and not as solutions to their issues. They would likely become more upset and ask further questions. When asked many questions, you will feel you are being judged or criticized and become upset yourself. Then you may accuse them of being insecure or nosy, which could lead to an argument.

Bear in mind, however, that people do not ask questions in this manner to intentionally hurt you. Many times they are unaware of doing so. People are simply attempting to get their needs met and solve their problems. They are dependent on you to help solve their problem, which neither of you may realize. So, they ask you questions to help solve their problem and to _get their needs met_. But your answers will not meet their needs. Why? _Because their needs are problems that they want to get resolved._ _You hear the questions, not the needs._ If you become defensive or give excuses, this does not satisfy the person's needs or issue. This, in turn, causes them to become more upset and ask even more questions, which intensifies the problem and makes things worse.

Upset people who ask such questions are actually using them like weapons or "bolts of passive anger" against you, which causes you to feel verbally attacked. Each "bolt of passive anger" thrown at you releases their frustration, but causes you pain or discomfort. Their aim is not really to hurt you, but an expression of their own hurt or needs not being met. The person has a problem, but using questions as "bolts of passive anger" will not solve the problem.

Instead of answering questions in such situations, what should you do? Find out what the person really wants from you. Again, use an acknowledgment statement first (i.e. giving the person credit for their questions), immediately followed by Direct Anger: telling the person to give you more information. This acknowledgment followed by direct anger is an automatic shield to the "bolts of anger" directed at you. Now you're in a position to help the person solve his/her problem. The results?

o Improved communication.
o A strengthening of the relationship.
o Avoidance of a hassle or argument.

Summary: Let us emphasize that you don't answer question only when you feel pressure or anxiety. If you resist questions all of the time, people will begin to resent you or see you as hostile or difficult. Questions are a valid part of life and communication. Do answer questions, of course, as part of your normal daily interaction with people and in non-pressure situations. However, as soon as you feel pressure or any anxiety, neither answer nor ask any questions.

"HTE"

Another important point: If you feel *pressure* or *anxiety* about any question, even the first question, *don't* _answer or ask any questions_. Simply acknowledge the question and tell the person to explain _why_ they are asking that. (_Tell_ them to explain, but don't ask a question).

We call this "HTE" - "Have Them Explain." After you have acknowledged their question, use Direct Anger, (an instructional statement) and _tell_ them to tell you more about what they want to know or why they are asking. This achieves two important objectives:

1. It helps to dilute the other person's aggression towards you.
2. It keeps you in control of you life space.
   a. It also provides security for the other and prevents you from taking on the other person's problem.

All of these benefits make things easier for you without offending the other person. However, only do this if you feel pressure or anxiety about the question. If you don't feel this, it is not necessary to use "HTE."

Usually those who ask the questions are trying to gain control of their feelings of insecurity. This is not necessarily negative. The person may or may not be in a negative mood. Sometimes it is important that a person ask questions to take control, and we love it. For example, if a group becomes totally lost in the woods, one person may ask questions in order to get a bearing as to where the group is, etc. The person may ask for certain landmarks, etc. Questions in these situations are welcome by others because they feel someone is in charge, which helps reduce anxiety and increase feelings of hope that things will turn out all right. In this illustration, the questions are not designed to have a "negative" impact on people or to prove them wrong, etc. Questions used in this scenario are designed to get information to try to rescue everyone from the woods.

From another perspective, let's look at the use of questions in a classroom environment, which are part of the students learning process. Questions create pressure because they are designed to change the student by imparting new knowledge. Questions asked by teachers are designed to control the learning process of the students. With a final exam, especially, there is a tremendous amount of anxiety on the students part. They need to answer questions correctly (as many as possible) to show how much they actually learned. The use of questions, however, in this context has a positive effect - to enhance knowledge. However, in terms of using our approach to get what you want, avoid questions when you feel pressured or uncomfortable in a conversation. If people ask tons of questions, continual arguments may ensue - especially if questions are asked as a challenge to another's integrity or character. Questions which begin with: "Why don't you.....", "Can't you ever.....", "Why do you always.....", etc., are not designed to elicit information. They are usually asked to provoke an argument or reveal hostility. These type of questions are a form of passive hostility. They are used to try to control others, to manipulate their responses, to coerce them, or try to force them to say things they don't really mean.

That is why when you ask people a series of questions in a row, they become defensive, and the questioner will seldom get what he or she wants with any consistency. Further, when a person asks many questions, it often indicates a lack of clarity as to what they want. Typically, no matter what your answers are, you will get more questions. Once you answer the first question, more follow. The series of questions make most people feel encroached upon and they become defensive. This impedes healthy and productive communication.

Tips on Not Asking and Not Answering Questions

o Not Asking Questions. This one is easier because all you have to do is <u>not</u> ask questions. You simply replace your questions (passive anger) with an instructional statement (direct anger). For example, if you wanted to know why someone had asked you a question you would <u>tell them:</u>

    a. "Tell me why you are asking that."
    b. "Explain what you are asking me."
    c. "Help me to understand what you are asking."

Giving instructions (direct anger) keeps you in control of how people enter into your life space. It also reduces the chances of your feelings being hurt or creating an argument.

o Not Answering Questions. This provides somewhat more of a challenge because we are more conditioned to answering questions. Phrases to use to avoid answering questions:

    a. "Let me think about that."
    b. "That's a good question. I'm glad you brought that up."
    c. "That's a good point. Thanks for telling me that."
    d. "Hold your questions and tell me more about your issue."

After using one of these phrases, use instructions (direct anger) and <u>tell</u> the person to give you more information. Not answering questions keeps you from being manipulated, pressured, or set up to be proved wrong on a point.

Control Your Life Space

Let's examine how to use these phrases in conjunction with instructions (direct anger). If you feel anxious or threatened by a question, instead of answering, use direct anger to have them tell you more about their issue. First, give the person credit for their question. Then, give them instructions: tell them to give you information so you can make a decision.

For example: If you are asked: "Does your spouse boss you around?" Instead of being offended by the implication, acknowledge what the person said by responding: "I didn't think you were going to ask such a question." This statement has a neutralizing effect on the questioner without offending him or her. Then take charge of your life space with the following instructional statement, "Tell me why you are asking that." This is direct anger: It directs the person to provide you information and reveal their intent.

The person may be persistent, due to their feelings of insecurity about that issue, and may aggressively or offensively respond: "Answer the question!" Don't get nervous or give in even if you feel tempted to do so. Respond:

a. "I can see this means a lot to you."
b. "I can see how you have a lot of energy with this."

These are effective phrases which acknowledge what the person is saying and prevent them from continuing their verbal attack. They recognize the person's point and essentially gives credit for it. The person feels accepted, which virtually disarms them. Thus, they have less need to be aggressive or offensive because they feel understood.

These are examples of taking control of your life space. Follow-up with an instructional statement (direct anger). Examples:

1. "Tell me why this is important to you."
2. "Explain what it is that you want to know from me."

3. "Tell me why you are saying that."
4. "Give me more information about that."

These phrases keep you in control of your own life space as well as in charge of the conversation. Such phrases also provide <u>stability</u> for the other person and reduce their feelings of insecurity, which makes things easier for you.

<u>Mixed Angers</u>

As stated previously, people often mix direct anger with passive anger. "Answer the question!" is direct anger, a powerful form of anger. But if the tone is aggressive or offensive, this is passive or indirect anger - which is a weak or dependent type of anger. So they have mixed two angers - direct and passive. Passive anger reveals both insecurity and dependency and tries to force or coerce you to answer in a certain way. Recognize the person's insecurity; then use an acknowledgment statement followed immediately by a direct anger statement.

This process automatically provides some security for this insecure person, which then neutralizes and reduces their drive to be aggressive or offensive. It also avoids a quarrel or an argument with that person. One final point: If you succumb to the temptation to answer the question, you set yourself up for more questions and, perhaps, judgments about yourself. Moreover, your answers may well be used against you later in the conversation to prove you wrong. So, stay focused on using instructional statements (Direct

Anger) - **Take the positive and healthy route - Direct Anger.**

Chapter 4

The Value of Being Independent

Avoid Being Dependent On Other People - Know What You Want

We are all initially dependent beings. We emerge naked from our mother's womb, where it is nice and warm and safe, and enter this world essentially defenseless. As infants, we depend on our parent or guardian to do everything for us: to clothe us and keep us warm, to feed us so we do not starve, to change our dirty diapers and help us to feel comfortable, etc. We are totally dependent at this point. Later, as we develop, we start to learn how things work and begin to help ourselves. We are taught, by our parent, guardian, by teachers at school, or simply through experience, how to do things for ourselves and become more independent. Eventually, we arrive at the point where we are essentially fully independent and can do most things for ourselves. Regardless of how experienced we are or how independent we may become at doing things and helping ourselves, our innate nature pulls us toward dependency.

Given a choice, virtually all of us would prefer to be dependent. (i.e., have other people figure things out for us and automatically do things for us without us having to tell people what to do). This is almost an automatic reflex. Dependency is not totally negative - sometimes there is the element of surprise (i.e., people doing something we'd hoped they'd do or give us something we'd hoped we'd get). Dependency is when a person wants, needs, or expects something from others, without telling them your expectations. Although we may like being dependent, it can create problems for us when our needs are not met. Then we feel hurt, which is an unpleasant feeling.

Dependency Examined

How is dependency defined in terms of how it is used in this book? Dependency is defined as wanting, needing, or expecting something from others without specifically stating what we expect. This includes wanting the other person to *intuitively* know what you want, to give you what you want, or do things for you without you *directly communicating* them to the person.

Often, we think others should automatically know what we want from them. And when they do not give us what we want, we become upset. We fail to realize that others are busy trying to satisfy their own needs. They, in turn, may wonder why we are not giving them what they want - which may explain their resistance to us. Both parties feel the other should know their respective wants without those being communicated. This occurs in virtually all relationships.

We must first stop believing the other person intuitively knows what we want or what we feel. If we don't, we'll invariably be disappointed and frustrated, believing the other person does not care for us. This issue is often the basis for arguments with couples. When their partner does not respond as they wish, each goes around in circles, trying to figure out the other person.

Often we hear the following statements:

1. "They knew that I did not want them to do that."
2. "They should have known that I wanted them to do that."
3. "They've known me long enough to know I would not like that."

All reasonable statements, right? Yes, but they reveal that the speaker is in a dependent role. To enjoy a successful relationship, avoid the dependency role. Take responsibility and tell the other person what, how, and when to do things for you. The more specific you are, the better you'll feel and the other person will clearly know what you want and what to do for you. Thus, they too will feel better.

Let us illustrate with a story. A client had a positive six-year relationship with her boyfriend. She praised herself for phoning him four or five times a week and dating regularly. When she moved to a new apartment, she felt she wanted him to take more initiative and call <u>her</u> more often. Instead of telling him this, she simply stopped calling him and waited for him to call her. He thought she had lost interest and felt rejected. Both had made assumptions about the other person instead of communicating their needs. Both resisted this for fear of failure or rejection.

We are all dependent on other people for a variety of needs - from basic physical needs to emotional, psychological, and intellectual needs. Since we have dependency in many of life's situations, we need to control our dependency. Dependency, in and of itself, is not bad. But we must control how things or people enter our life space. We must take charge and be responsible for ourselves. The more we take control of how others enter our life space, the happier we will be and the more successful (and happy) others will be as well.

<u>Roots of Dependency</u>

Dependency stems from infancy onwards. As children, we depended on our parents for virtually everything. We felt parents could solve all our problems. However, as we grew older, the ability of our parents to solve problems seemed to vanish. But in reality, it never really vanished. What really happened was we developed our own character, personality, goals, lifestyles, etc. The solutions to our problems had to match our personality, lifestyle choices, character traits, etc. The truth is we must solve problems in a way that harmonizes with our individuality. The solutions to problems must fit our particular personality. Parents may offer answers to our problems that are more in harmony with their own personality, choices, goals, individuality, etc. Therefore, as children grow and confront more complex problems, parents encourage their children to solve their own problems themselves.

Dependency issues need to be addressed especially when our problems become more personal and complex and we face multiple choices. We have to solve problems in a way that best suits our particular temperament and lifestyle. Further, the answer to our problems must also fit our particular situation and within the context of who we are and what we need. There is no one "correct" or "right" answer to a problem. What is "right" for one person may be "wrong" for someone else. The ultimate decision rests with each of us. We cannot depend on someone else to know what we want. Nor can we revert to the role of being a child, where our parents solved our problems for us. We must solve our own problems in our own special individual ways.

Know What You Want

In order to avoid being dependent on others, and become independent, we must first decide what we want. Then _help_ the other person to know _how_ to give that to you. How? Again, you use direct anger. If we are not sure about exactly what we want, _guess_! This may sound peculiar at first. The important point is we must act. If our first guess is not what we really want, guess again until the answer or solution feels right. As you begin to get closer to the solution that will work best for you, your anxiety will begin to subside. When this happens, you'll know you've arrived at the best solution for you. In certain situations, you may have to do research first to discover what you truly want. As you gather information, you'll be in a better position to make the best decision for yourself - that which best suit your individual needs.

Let us give you a very brief example of how this works. A woman wants to see a movie but does not want to go alone. She calls her boyfriend. He's not available until much later. Initially she agrees, but then changes her mind. She calls her best friend. Her best friend wants to see a different film. The woman again agrees, but then changes her mind again; that solution did not feel right either. She decides to invite her sister. Her sister suggests an old movie redone in color presented on the big screen. This solution feels right. She decides to go. Her anxiety about what to do is gone. The woman had to keep guessing trying to determine what she really wanted to do until she found something that felt right for her. When she found that solution, that is what she did.

Focus On Your Wants

Many people have stated they feel uncomfortable guessing what it is they want. In their minds, they fear that people will view their "guessing" as being "wishy washy" or indecisive. Resist this type of thinking! This fear represents your being dependent on other people. As we try to think about what others believe or feel, we cannot be actively involved in solving or finding the proper solutions to our own problems. We must focus on what we want, need, or think. If someone accuses you of being indecisive or "wishy washy," avoid the temptation to respond defensively. Simply say, "Let me be "wishy-washy." When people state their opinion, it usually represents their attempt to please you and help you out. But if you keep changing your mind, the person would get confused and not know how to please you. This would block their progress in trying to help you and cause them to criticize.

To help them with this, give them directions about how to respond to you. For example, if someone accuses you of being indecisive, reply: "I know it may seem like I am indecisive, but let me be this way and go along with me. I'd really like that." Then the other person knows how to please and is not confused. It helps relieve their anxiety of reacting to your decision-making process, (i.e., your guessing process). They will feel better when you tell them how to please you.

Remember, people love pleasing others. Even your enemies love pleasing you. You help people to please you when you clarify what you want them to do for you and how you want them to do it. When you give clear instructions (direct anger), people will feel successful with you and like you more.

There is a reverse side to this. When you tell a person what <u>not</u> to do, or what they have done wrong, or what they *should* have done, they will feel you disapprove of them and want to change them. Inevitably, most people will rebel, become defensive, and find fault with you. Then both of you may become defensive and hence, dependent. Both of you then waste time justifying or defending your respective positions. Eventually, each of you may become irritated and insults or an argument may ensue, which could escalate into a full scale argument.

The ultimate cause of this type of situation? Neither of you knew what you wanted because you were *dependent* on the other person. Each person waited for the other person to verbalize their own needs. Each person failed to take responsibility for her or his own needs being met; then helping the other person meet those needs. Use direct anger to act and react in an independent way. You never try to change, pressure or force others to do anything for you. You simply instruct (tell) others what to do for you.

One final point. To avoid being dependent on other people, want things *for yourself*, not for the other person. For example, a relative of ours had marital problems. We told him to decide what *he* wanted. He said that he wanted to know *what she wanted*. This only added more confusion.

The want we are talking about is a want for yourself and _only_ for yourself, exclusive of the other person's want or desire. Your want must be _independent_ of what the other person thinks. Your want must come solely from yourself. We told our relative to forget what his wife wanted (because he could never know that with any certainty) and to decide _only_ what he wanted _for himself_. What our relative _really wanted_ was to get back together with his wife in order to solve their problems together. His clear _want_ was identified and based solely on what he wanted. Now he could decide _when_ he got what he wanted and could then help his spouse accomplish what he wanted. If he insisted on focusing on knowing what his wife wanted, he would have never gotten what _he_ really wanted - which ultimately benefited both.

Avoid Trying to "Program" People

What does it mean to "program people?" To irrationally attempt to force or coerce a person to respond in a certain way every time; the way that you want them. In so doing, when a situation arises you depend on them to behave or react in that certain way. You want them to do this despite their own needs, wants, and feelings. If they don't react as you wish, sooner or later you'll feel disappointed. Why? Because the person would eventually have to deal with his or her own needs, pressures, wants, etc. Essentially, this concept is similar to trying to program someone as you would a computer.

Don't program people to do what you want.

If others had to deal with one of their own issues, you'd expect them interact with you as programmed. Then you'd feel upset at them for not acting as you programmed them to do. In intimate relationships, eventually relationship problems develop. Each person feels their own needs are not being met.

Instead of increasing the potential for involvement in unpleasant or uncomfortable situations, don't try to program people! Take the responsibility _each and every_ time to tell people what and how to do things for you by using direct anger statements. It is absolutely important that you take full responsibility for getting what you want from others. We cannot depend on others to ensure that our needs are met. Even if we are "successful" in programming a person to behave in a certain way, our needs may eventually change. If your needs change and the other person continues to behave as programmed, they would then fail to meet your new needs. In order for others to meet your needs, and for you to avoid dependency by trying to program people, always tell them clearly what to do for you by using direct anger statements.

Let us use one of the examples illustrated earlier: In this example, John wanted Bob to call him every Tuesday night at 7:30 p.m., John should have used direct anger (instructional statements) and avoided any threats or manipulations. This taps into a person's desire to please and stimulates them to want to please you. John might have said, "Call me every Tuesday night at 7:30 p.m. I'd appreciate hearing from you then." This simple direct anger (instructional) statement, gives clear and concise instructions and also informs others what makes you happy. Notice it does not manipulate, threaten, or force the other person. The latter part of the statement taps into their desire to please you - and will please themselves as well.

Instead of succumbing to dependency needs, use direct anger (instructional statement). For example, you may instruct the person to do something for you -- (i.e. tell them to apologize to you for letting you down, or talk with you about another way to handle this calling situation, or tell them to explain what prevented them from calling you, etc. This may sound controlling, but it's not. You are clarifying what you want in a way which conveys they have the right to do it or not. Whatever you do, don't allow upset feelings to depress you. Remember, you cannot program a person to do things for you each and every time and then depend on them to do it. If they don't come through for you, deal with that situation when it happens. It may sound cumbersome to tell others to do something for you each·time they let you down. But, it has a positive effect. It keeps you from being dependent on the other person.

You can depend on others to do things for you only when <u>you control</u> your dependency needs. You control your dependency needs by <u>not</u> trying to program the person. Again, use direct anger to tell the person what to do for you and the importance that issue has to you. This keeps you independent and puts you in control of your happiness.

<u>Be Independent</u>

To program someone to do things is an example of coercion, which negates their <u>desire</u> to please you. They may do as you want, but they will harbor resentment. When you rob a person's desire to please, it makes them unhappy.

Expecting others to automatically know what you want is dependency. Most often, these type of dependency needs will not be met by others. Don't expect others to automatically know what you want. Be independent! Use Direct Anger statements. Decide what you want and then help the other person to satisfy that need. When a person makes a conscious decision to do what you want them to do, they act from their "free will;" they've decided it pleases them and they <u>want</u> to do it. Their desire to please you makes them feel good.

Summary: Trying to program people always creates problems. The person being programmed is burdened with an extra responsibility they may not be able to fulfill <u>every time</u>. The person trying to program is essentially <u>threatening</u> or <u>manipulating</u> the other person. Further, the person doing the programming is in a dependent position. Dependency, as defined here, creates an unnecessary and unhealthy burden for everyone involved.

Chapter 5

Analyzing the Other Person - and Yourself

When you use the "Lewis Approach" to get what you want, the ability to analyze others is virtually essential. Does this mean you need to research a host of psychological principles? That is too complicated and time consuming. There are relatively simple things to listen for when talking with a person to determine one's motivation behind behavior. In effect, to analyze others is to *listen to the words* they use, determine the emotions they feel, and then measure the impact of their emotions on you and on themselves. By analyzing the other person, you will be in a much better position to understand the other's state of mind. Thus, you will know what to say to deal more effectively with that person.

At first, such analysis may sound difficult and uninviting. We know some people well and others not so well. Sometimes those we know well may begin to act differently with us; this makes analyzing them as challenging as analyzing those we don't know as well. Whether you know the person or not, analyzing others is relatively simple.

Basically, the human mind works only one way! Whenever there is a change or crisis in our lives, we get angry, consciously or subconsciously. Anger helps us to adjust to the change or crisis. When that anger is expressed either favorably or negatively, an element of guilt inevitably ensues. The guilt has to be dealt with somehow. We may become dependent on others to help, but fail to communicate what we want. This period of change or crisis can last for <u>up to</u> six weeks before being finally resolved, good or bad. This is the basic workings of the mind in virtually all types of people and in all types of cultures. Recognizing this fact of human nature helps to make analyzing the other person easier.

At different times people have different emotions. They may handle one situation one way at certain times, a different way other times. When a person first awakens in the morning, one attitude may be dominant, and a different attitude arise after a cup of coffee. If a person has had a bad day or experienced disappointments, he or she may have bad feelings and be more abrupt. But, if that same person had a good day and things went well, he or she would be in a much happier frame of mind.

We all experience these mood changes. Our responses to people may vary based on how the particular circumstances of our lives affect us at a certain point in time. Often, people are not even aware of how their situations affect their moods. Therefore, it is very difficult to recognize our own mood, demeanor, or state of mind at any specific time. Even a person who is in a good mood may be affected negatively by our words and become angry. We are all aware subconsciously of how other people act towards us and we make judgments and determinations based on that. In fact, we all tend to analyze people generally without really thinking about it.

How To Analyze Effectively

There are simple and effective ways to analyze people to help you successfully interact better with them. This is why analyzing is so valuable.

Firstly, be aware that most of us undergo various changes throughout, which require us to make adjustments. To some extent, every change represents stress. In terms of analyzing others, when a person is stressed, try to pinpoint the change that occurred. This may account for that person's stress level.

Stress also has a positive aspect: it helps us to adapt to the change. To help you determine what the change is, state: "Tell me why you are dealing with that now." (Note: This is a direct anger statement, using the action verb, "Tell"). This helps to determine what change may have triggered the stress. Especially be aware of that which is new. In particular, look for changes when interacting with those who are aggressive, upset, pressuring you, questioning you, and so forth.

As stated earlier, there are a few specific ways to analyze others. The primary ones presented in this book include: A. How not to take on another person's problem. B. Recognizing the "8 Feet Rule." C. Recognizing "I" and "You" words.

Don't "Take On" Another Person's Problem

We get most into trouble with people, or cause discomfort, when we take on another person's problem. We do this so often, we are not even aware of it. This is a very easy trap, because it is so tempting. How can you recognize when you have taken on another person's problem? The test is simple: If you approach a person feeling in a good mood and leave feeling negative, uncomfortable, or defensive, you have assumed their problem.

Taking on another person's problem occurs when you are being blamed, accused or pressured. You may or may not be at fault. But if you become defensive, explain your position, or become involved with the solution, you have assumed the person's problem.

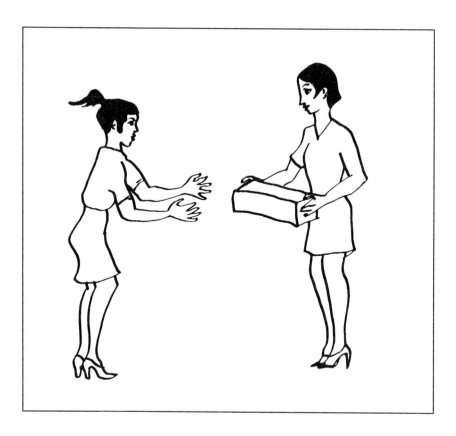

<u>Unlike</u> the woman above, don't take on another person's problem.

For example, if someone said that you caused them to miss their lunch because you ate all of the food in the refrigerator and, assuming you did eat the food, you would now be set up to take on that person's problem. Now you have to explain or defend your position. Or you may blame them for not planning their lunch better. Now the other person feels criticized or pressured, even though your intent is to help them solve their problem. If you explain, defend, or blame the person, you have fallen into the trap of taking on someone else's problem. Do you ignore what the person says? No. That would be being negative selfish and at the other person's expense.

What is at the root of this tendency to take on another person's problem? Consciously or subconsciously, we sense the other person's insecurity and dependence on us. When their needs are not getting met, people tend to focus on you as the cause of their un-fulfillment. Usually this is not justified. It often happens when people are angry about something unrelated to you. They may lash out at you and later apologize. Even if you become involved with their lashing at you, you have also taken on the other person's problem.

Instinctively, we want to defend ourselves and prevent people from accusing or verbally attacking us. To avoid unpleasantness, hassles, and trouble with others, don't take on another person's problem! We're all responsible for solving our own problems. Of course, we can be supportive and understand their problem. But allow others the freedom to deal with their own problems.

We have developed two ways to avoid taking on other people's problems. Use our concept called "HTE": "Have Them Explain." (discussed previously in a different situation). Tell the person: "Be Nicer To Me." Each of these can be used in a variety of situations.

"HTE." Essentially, here you instruct the person to tell you <u>why</u> they are saying what they are. If a person is rude or verbally attacks, blames, or pressures you, give the person instructions. Tell them to tell you why they are speaking to you in that manner. Examples:

    A. "Tell me more about the problem."
    B. "Explain to me the reason you brought that to my attention."
    C. "Tell me why this is important for you to take the time to go over this."

These are direct anger statements. To use "HTE" properly, you must tell or instruct people what to do for you. By using direct anger (instructional statements), don't ask questions. If you ask questions, confront, or challenge their behavior or manner of speaking, you are using passive anger, which does not work. As stated before, passive anger is a weak and ineffective anger. Don't ask questions when using "HTE." Use only statements and instructions, (i.e. direct anger). By using "HTE," you help the person to focus on his or her problem, paving the way for the person to find a solution, as opposed to dumping on you. If you simply ask questions, they may not address their problem or be stimulated to change how or what they are telling you. Their verbal attack on you may continue.

Additionally, when you use "HTE" by utilizing direct anger statements, people feel that you care about their issue. They are then less motivated to continue their verbal attack on you. Thus, it becomes easier for you to not take on their problem.

Another important point in using "HTE" is: How many times do you tell the person to explain? Once, twice, or ten or fifteen times? Generally, you use "HTE" until you do not feel any pressure from them. As a practical guide, you may tell them to explain up to three times. The first time, tell them to explain <u>why</u> they are saying what they are. The second time, tell them to explain <u>how</u> the issue is bothering them. The third time, tell them to explain <u>what</u> they propose as a solution.

One more point: Notice what you have done so far. The person originally started by accusing, blaming, or pressuring you. They have essentially verbally attacked you to some degree. And you have used "HTE" to instruct them to give you more information. You told them to tell you the **why**, **how**, and **what** of their issue. The person has followed your instructions without being aware of this. The significance is: <u>You are in control of the flow of the conversation</u>. The main benefit is that you have <u>stopped</u> their verbal attack on you by using direct anger. This helps the person focus on his or her own problem and seek a solution. More importantly, you have avoided taking on the other person's problem - without aggravating the person.

After you have used the last step of "HTE," they may offer a proposal that you are willing to accept. If you do that, the situation is concluded. You have thus successfully kept yourself from taking on the other person's problem, protected yourself from verbal abuse, and have helped the person solve his or her own problem.

If, however, the person makes a proposal you do not like, then use direct anger to instruct them to give you other choices. Again, this keeps you from taking on the other person's problem. It also keeps the other person focused on doing all of the work to solve his or her own problem. Keep using this process until the person gives you a choice that you can accept. If the person does not become more reasonable, and you do not wish to spend more time on the topic, tell them to change their request, or tell them to let you think about it, etc. Use some kind of direct anger statement that *instructs* them to do something for you. The key point is never take on another person's problem. Instead, keep using "HTE." Life presents enough problems for us without our having to be manipulated or coerced into taking on other people's problems as well. "HTE" is the best way to avoid this and allows you to feel less pressured and more comfortable. It has a positive double impact: You both experience relief and the other person is focused on his or her problem and helped to solve it.

By not taking on the person's problem, you are in a position to help the person solve their problem in a way that is more satisfying.

The other concept is to say: "Be nicer to me." Use this when someone insults, criticizes, or is rude to you - whether the person is aware or not of their abusive behavior. Many times, people say things to try to help you unaware they are actually bothering or hurting you. The direct anger statement, "Be nicer to me." tells people to treat you better without offending them.

If someone insults, criticizes, or is rude to you, recognize that the person has a problem and their problem is not yours. Again, don't take on that person's problem. Admittedly, this is hard to do. In such situations, our automatic response is to protect ourselves, either by defending ourselves or verbally attacking the other person. Again, to do so is to fall into the trap of <u>taking on the other person's problem</u>. Further, you have also given the other person *power over* you! Why? You have allowed them to *dictate* your reactions and your feelings. This, essentially, puts the other person in control when they are unable to assume control.

For example, you are lying on the couch watching TV and your friend enters the room, looks at you, and exclaims: "You know, you are too fat." Even if you are overweight, does their remark add any weight to your body? No. So, clearly, this weight thing is not your problem, it's theirs. To deal with this situation, use "Be nicer to me."

First, determine if their comment bothered you (i.e., did you feel insulted or criticized?) Most of us would determine this did bother us. If so, use "Be nicer to me." This tells the person they are being critical of you and quickly lets them know <u>what</u> you want them to do for you. You tell them <u>what</u> to do for you rather than what <u>not</u> to do. This clear message does not pressure or challenge the other person.

To go one step further, when you use "Be Nicer To Me," the person may become defensive and say : "I was only trying to help you; telling you that for your own good." At this point, you are still in charge of the conversation. The person is freely explaining themselves to you. This is what typically happens when you use "Be Nicer To Me."

What is your reply after they explain themselves? Give the person credit for what they said and then use direct anger. Reply: "Thanks for thinking of me. But be nicer to me. I'd appreciate that." Giving the person credit for what they say will reduce their motivation to criticize. The direct anger is: "Be nicer to me." This instructs others as to what you want them to do for you, without verbally attacking them or needing to defend yourself. This gives you a tremendous advantage: It keeps you protected and avoids hassles or arguments. More importantly, you remain in *control* of your life space. Our own experiences, and those with whom we have worked, have shown this to be very effective and successful.

The "8 Feet Rule"

Before we get into the specifics of the "8 Feet" rule, let us tell you how this came about. In high school, Charles Sr.'s played track and field, and was one of the fastest guys in Los Angeles in the 1950's. While on the field, one of the events he liked was the high jump. A few guys came close to clearing 7 feet, but no one could clear 8 feet. In order for those few to jump that high, the bar had to be lowered to what they could jump; then slowly and gradually raised to that height. This is how we created the "8 Feet" concept, which we have applied in our approach to getting what you want.

The "8 Feet" rule helps you to recognize when you are asking a person to do something they cannot do, (i.e. jumping "8 Feet" for you). When you direct others to give you what you want with words, sometimes you won't get what you want initially, or at all. Why? It may be beyond their capacity; this represents "8 Feet" for the other person. So, this rule helps you to determine if it is beyond their capacity or not. And it provides you with the steps to help them give you what you want, or come as close as possible.

The "8 Feet Rule" can be very helpful. Knowing about the "8 Feet Rule" allows you to determine what the other person's capacity is toward pleasing you. Thus, you avoid feeling rejected or angry if others are unable to jump the "8 Feet". You gain the ability to see whether they have the capacity to jump the "8 Feet", or if they simply don't want to comply, which could represent hostility.

Using the "8 Feet Rule" helps the person to jump "8 Feet" by "lowering the bar." Then you slowly raise it to get as close as possible to what you want them to do. One of the best benefits of using the "8 Feet Rule" is that it gives <u>you</u> the ability to guide the person toward being a success with you! This makes them feel better and pleases you as well.

By lowering the bar from "8 Feet," you allow the person to be a success with you and "clear the bar." You can then slowly raise the bar back toward "8 Feet," guiding them to please you.

People like pleasing others. If you are using our approach and someone is not coming through for you, two things may be preventing this: 1. They may not know <u>how</u> to do what you want them to do. 2. They may not have the <u>ability</u> to do what you want them to do. These are really the only two reasons.

If person does not <u>know</u> how or does not have the <u>ability</u> to do what you want at the time you instruct them, they will not be able to clear "8 Feet" for you.

Let's look at these two situations. Let's say you want someone who has baked before to bake a marbled fudge cake for you. But, using our approach, they resist. You would be disappointed and feel, perhaps, they didn't like you or were angry. You then tell the person to tell you why they resist, adding it means a lot to you. The person might reveal that they have never baked a marbled fudge cake and they felt nervous about doing so. What has happened? You learned the truth of their resistance: they did not know how to bake this type of cake.

The "8 Feet" rule helped you to identify this. You learned the real issue and that their resistance was not personal. At this point, if you still wanted the person to bake the cake for you, tell the person to do the best they can with the marbled fudge cake or to bake another kind of cake. This represents you "lowering the bar" to a height to match the person's capacity.

Now let's focus on those who may not have the ability to give you what you want. For example, you asked a friend for a loan, stating you'd repay it in a month. But the friend resists. Have your friend to tell you what is getting in the way of his doing so. He may say he needs the money for his educational needs. At this point, you recognize he may not be able to "jump" that high for you. Notice he is not blaming you or judging you; he is telling you about his own issue. Now, you have a choice: Are you willing to accept your friend's decision or is the loan more important to you. If you are willing to accept your friend's decision, you thank him for considering it. If, however, the loan is still important to you, you might reply: "I understand about your school and I am glad you shared that with me. But the loan means a lot to me. Work something out so that you can lend me the money anyway. I'd really appreciate that." If the person agreed, you'd have successfully helped him to "jump 8 feet" for you. They would have done something for you to make you happy, which they were not willing to do initially. Further, they will feel happy because they have chosen, out of their "free will" (minus any force, criticism, manipulation, etc.) to give you the loan. In essence, they would have decided to please themselves.

By using direct anger and stressing the importance your
issue has to you, people will be more motivated to want to
please you. This often results in them jumping "8 Feet"
and doing what you want.

If, however, the person does not give you the loan,
the person may not be able to jump that high for you at this
time. What might you do? You could lower the bar; have
them tell you if there are other things they can do to help
you with your situation. You might say: A. "Tell me if
there is something you can do to help me out with this." B.

"I'd really appreciate you working something out to help me in any way that you are able." These two statements "lower the bar" for the person.

When you do this, people <u>love</u> to do things for you. Many times they will offer very creative ways to help you and come as close as they can to do what you asked. This really motivates the person to <u>want</u> to help you. Why? Using this process, you have avoided making the other person feel uncomfortable. You focused only on <u>giving the person instructions</u> as to how to please you.

Another point in relation to the "8 Feet Rule:" always honor people's "free will," their right to refuse you. Give people the right to say "no". However, you can use our approach to greatly *increase* the number of times when people say "yes," even if they have initially said "no." (See "Getting Though Resistance")

Another point to be aware of using the "8 Feet Rule." If a person refuses you, based on what you may have said or done, do not feel you are the source of the person's problem. Your behavior or personality traits do not preclude others from doing what you want. Others are responsible for their own emotions. For example, if a person refuses to drive you somewhere, because of your lateness on a previous engagement, this indicates his or her own reaction, disappointment, or issue. They may not want to experience another frustration arising from your lateness. Deal with the situation now: their refusal to drive you. Don't shift the focus. Don't allow yourself to be manipulated by having to explain or justify your past lateness. This will cause you to focus on the other person's issue at the expense of your own. These types of situations cause many people to become upset.

Resist these tendencies. See things from another perspective: that you are not the source of a person's problem. Instead, have the person focus on what is getting in the way of them doing what you want <u>now</u>. This will help them focus on the real issue of their resistance (i.e. their emotions). When others work through their own problems, they will then be in a much better position to jump "8 Feet" for you and please you.

Before we move on to the next section, let us examine one more variation of this "8 feet" rule. A relative of ours once told us that when he used our approach, the person simply turned and walked away. Was this an example of "8 feet," he asked? Yes. This person was apparently not able to jump the "8 feet", so he tried to avoid it all together. What can you do? If you go after the person walking away, you are being aggressive or hostile, which could lead to negative circumstances and results. This is an intrusion of their space without their consent. You can do two things: A. <u>Tell them to let you walk with them</u> B. <u>Tell them to come back and talk to you</u>. By simply saying such words, people will often respond positively. Why does this work? By telling them to let you walk with them (a direct anger statement) or to "come back" (another direct anger statement), frees them to make their own decision. Their decision, whether positive or negative, is anger which empowers them. If they say no, that is anger. You might reply: "Change your mind for me." Or "Don't say no. Say yes." If they say yes, say "Thank you. I really appreciate that." Then continue with what you want to say.

Our experience has shown that using such simple "direct anger" statements work wonders with people! They respond positively, even when you think they won't. For further dialogue on this point, see section on "Comprehensive Examples".

"I" and "You" Words

"I" and "You" words is an concept Charles Jr. identified in the course of writing this book. Although it has always been a part of our approach, it is now organized more concisely, making it easier to recognize and to use.

Essentially, "I" and "you" words are indicators you can listen for to help you determine what the other person is communicating. They help to instantly guide you as to your response - to help the other person do what you want them to do.

"I" Words

"I" words in conversation express a message of sharing, caring, sincerity, responsibility, and clarity. They are an attempt for one to be closer emotionally. They also reveal the inner thinking of the person using the "I" words. Those who use "I" words commit themselves to their belief and, thus, are more receptive to be scrutinized as to their viewpoint. The "I" word person usually is secure enough to move emotionally closer to someone without fear of rejection. Such persons are generally able to protect themselves emotionally from being hurt by others. The truth is, if you feel strongly about your beliefs, you would feel confident enough to state your viewpoint freely without fear. Even if you later realized that your position is not correct, you would be secure enough to correct your viewpoint.

"I" words, when used expressing direct anger, take responsibility for getting your needs met. They talk about yourself and preclude judging, evaluating, or criticizing others. "I" words focus on yourself, which keeps you focused on helping the person do what you want them to do for you. Thus, "I" words are direct and strong. Another point: direct anger is also loving; loving to the person giving and loving to the person receiving.

"You" Words

"You" words, in conversation, express a message of distance and un-involvement. They are an attempt to separate oneself from another. They are also very judgmental, putting the receiver of the word "you" on the spot. "You" words are generally used in either confrontational, judgmental, or negative conversational situations, and almost always when blaming someone.

"You" words express passive anger. They do not take responsibility for getting your needs met; they judge someone or shift the attention to that person. They fail to play an <u>active</u> role in instructing a person as to what to do and are, therefore, passive and weak. Remember, passive anger is painful; painful to both the giver and receiver.

Further, "you" words do not reveal what the other person is thinking. As a general statement, "you" words are associated with blaming, criticizing, value judging, negativism, and so forth. If you catch yourself using "you" words, be aware that you are feeling insecure. Phrases which include the use of the word "you" when used negatively are:

o "<u>You</u> always do this to me."
o "<u>You</u> always want everything your way."
o "<u>You</u> have a low patience level."
o "<u>You</u> should have thought more before you did that."

There is, however, a positive aspect to "you" words. Although "you" words are overall negative, there are times when "you" words have a positive effect. Examples:

o "<u>You</u> are fun to be with."
o "<u>You</u> are a nice person."
o "<u>You</u> did a good job."
o "<u>You</u> are next in line."

Although these positive comments are judging in nature, they are acceptable because their intent is positive.

"I" vs. "You" Words

Let's explore the differences between "I" and "You" words. When you hear "I" words, you hear the loving part of the person, their sense of security and confidence. These words are sharing and non-threatening; allowing you the freedom to share back without the fear of being hurt. Conversely, when you hear "you" words, you hear the insecurity, pain, and anger of the other person directly toward you. This puts you on the defensive, and makes you feel unsafe in sharing with the other person. A typical conversation to illustrate this:

Lydia: "Frank, you never think about me. You only think of yourself."

Frank: "You don't think about me! You didn't even say "Hi" to my mother when she came to visit."

This blaming discussion can continue indefinitely. Each person attacks the other, but neither gets what they want. Further, they both feel terrible and upset with the other.

Sometimes, both "I" and "You" words will be mixed into the conversation. For example: ""I" know you were trying to do the right thing, but "you" should have known better than to do that." And: "You" should have done it another way, although "I" understand what <u>you</u> were going through."

Let's examine the above dialog. All of the "I" words pose no threat to you, because they do not judge you. The "you" words, however, judge and criticize you. Even if what is said about "you" is correct, you'd still feel upset. Here, the 'you" words are designed to evaluate, criticize, and judge. Even if the speaker has no offensive intentions, you'd still feel bad, uncomfortable, or uneasy at that point.

Another point: If others use the word "I" often, such as: ""I" don't like this," ""I" don't like that," and especially if the "I" is followed by <u>an action verb</u> (direct anger), it is clear that the person is fairly independent and confident of what they want. The person is stable with their point of view. Statements which <u>reveal independence</u> begin with: "I saw," "I think," "I gave," or "I went," etc. These words also show clear direction and provide information. They show that a person can take a stand on issues and share ideas; that they are coming from a position of self-confidence.

On the other hand, when "I" is followed by a <u>passive verb</u> (passive anger): "I want," "I need," "I should," "I could," or "I wish," etc., this shows the person is less clear as to what they want. These <u>passive verbs</u> are dependent and weak: they don't give directions as to what to do or not to do. They do not give clear guidelines as to what the person wants to have happen. This reveals a dependent position.

Despite the issue of "<u>action verb</u>" versus "<u>passive verb</u>," the use of the word "I" is less threatening, more revealing, and clearer, than the use of the word "you".

Whenever you know exactly what you want, you present yourself as more secure, stable, and less threatening than those who do not know what they want. The analysis of "I" words followed by an <u>action verb</u> and "You" words followed by a <u>passive verb</u>, indicate where the person is coming from: i.e., independence and stability versus dependency and insecurity.

How To Analyze "I" Words and "You" Words

Using this analytical tool will benefit yourself and the other person as well. In conversation and when using our approach, use "I" words as much as possible. Be aware of "you" words when you feel uneasy or uncomfortable when conversing with another person. When instructing the other person to do what you want them to do for you, avoid "you" words. Use "I" words. How do you handle situations when someone is using "you" words with you? When you have problems or feel pressured about the "you" words you are hearing, start using the "Lewis Approach." People generally use "you" words when they feel insecure. If you are in a conversation, and you start hearing "you" words, or if you use "you" words yourself, this most likely means both parties feel insecure. However, refrain from verbalizing the other's insecurity because he or she will become defensive. Simply accept the fact that both of you are insecure.

What do you do in conversations when others use many "you" words? Firstly, be aware of the insecurity. Secondly, be aware that the person is dealing with his or her problem. Thirdly, and most importantly, don't take responsibility for another's problem. Give the person instructions using "<u>HTE</u>". Example: Other Person: "*You* were there and *you* didn't do anything." You: "*Tell* me what you mean." "*Explain* why you are saying that" "*Tell* me more about why you are saying that." Notice that we used the word "you" in our instruction statement (direct anger). The "you" was <u>not</u> used in a judging, threatening, or critical way, but only to obtain information. Bear in mind that the word "you" is not a problem in itself unless accompanied by a negative or judgmental statement. How to determine this? Simply by how you feel (i.e. If you feel uneasy or uncomfortable.)

A conversation between Mindy and Peter will illustrate how the "I" and "you" words work.

Mindy: "<u>You</u> never help around the house, <u>you</u> just take me for granted, then <u>you</u> come home at night and watch football and drink beer. <u>You're</u> lazy."

Peter: "Oh yeah, <u>you</u> think <u>you</u> do a lot, don't <u>you</u>? <u>You</u> don't have to go out there in traffic and deal with those crazy people. I think <u>you</u> got it easy and I don't like the way <u>you</u> nag me."

Mindy: "If _you_ think what I do is so easy why don't _you_ do this work here at home."

Peter: "_You're_ always nagging."

Clearly, both Mindy and Peter are angry and irritated with each other and are "dumping" on each other. They both reveal insecurity and dependency. But neither of them know how to get their respective needs met. Notice that in only two verbal exchanges, the word "you" was used 13 times, all with attacking type intentions.

Using the same example, assume Peter has read this book. How would his results with Mindy change?

Mindy: "_You_ never help around the house, _you_ just take me for granted, then _you_ come home at night and just watch football and drink beer. _You're_ lazy."

Peter: "Tell me why _you_ are saying these things to me." (Notice Peter is using "HTE").

Mindy: "Because _you're_ lazy and _you_ don't help me."

Peter: "I understand what _you_ are saying. But explain why _you_ are telling me this."

Mindy: "_You_ know why."

Peter: "I understand what _you_ said but tell me what _you_ are concerned about so I can know."

Mindy: "I have been doing all of the housework and then your mother called and wants me to take her shopping. I'm too busy to take her."

Peter: "Well, I understand that. Now I know what is bothering you."

This conversation would thus continue in a positive way, eventually concluding without an argument. By Peter focusing on "I" words and avoiding the use of "you" words, combined with using "HTE," Peter stood in a better position to help Mindy work out her own problem. Notice also that he did not take on her problem as his own. This allowed Mindy to keep her problem and solve it herself. In this conversation, we learned that her real problem was not Peter, but Peter's mother, who interfered with Mindy's work. Notice that although the word "you" was used about the same amount of times, Peter did not use it with attacking-type intentions. He used his "you's" neutrally, while all of Mindy's were attacking.

If you follow this positive concept, Mindy, in this case, would begin to tell Peter more and more about what is really bothering her. As a result, instead of creating an argument and feeling upset with each other, they'd achieve a better understanding of the problem and, therefore, have a better chance to successfully solve it. You will quickly find that this concept, recognizing and utilizing "I" and "you" words, will work for you by making problems easier to identify and determine who needs to solve them.

Summary: "I" words are much more effective when dealing with people. People will be more sharing, caring, and accepting of you. With "you" words, people feel that they are being criticized, judged, and distanced from you. Remember, however, that it is not the "you" word alone that causes problems. Only when they're used in an attacking, blaming, or accusatory-type manner. This will also help you to understand your situation and provide you with guidance as to what you can do to change it. You would change what you are doing (i.e. if you found yourself using accusatory-type "you" words, you'd switch to "I" words), or help the other person change what they are doing: If you observe the other person using "you" words, you would use "HTE" (direct anger statements) coupled with use of "I" words. This will guide you to make instant corrections and automatically help you, and the other person, to feel better and improve your conversation and/or your relationship together.

Chapter 6

Getting Through Resistance

Whenever you want someone to do anything for you, you often have to confront the other person's resistance initially. The person may need time to adjust to what you're saying before they can comply. People are frequently not aware they are resisting - which is a normal and natural response to change. In fact, resistance is part of their eventually doing what you want.

Change represents the unknown, to a certain degree, and thus we feel an increased chance of failing. We also fear disapproval. When we are instructing someone to do something for us, we are essentially instructing them to change something about themselves. Change is an inevitable part of life and people develop different ways to handle changes. Finding out how the person you are dealing with handles changes can be very helpful.

One way to determine this is to understand that they will ask you questions, an initial form of resistance. Charles Sr. noticed this in college; when the professor informed the class that they'd have a surprise quiz, the students immediately began to ask lots of questions: 1. "Is it true or false type questions?" 2. "Is it multiple choice?" 3. "How many questions will be on the quiz?" 4. "What weight will this have on our final grade?" These questions continued for close to twenty minutes. In retrospect, we realize that these students were simply resisting change, i.e., the unknown, a surprise quiz. Their questions revealed concern about whether they would pass or fail, give the correct answers, or be rejected if they failed the quiz, etc.

A second way to determine how a person handles change is: Notice how often they use negative words, such as: "I don't ...", "I hate...", "I can't ...", etc. Also notice if the person uses a lot of "You" words, which then reveals insecurity or uncertainty. Obviously, people who are insecure don't handle change very well.

Consider as well that some are more prepared for change than others. Some people have developed better coping skills to deal with change. In the example of the students, certain students may have read all of the required chapters covered in the quiz. Thus, the surprise quiz would be less of an unknown for them, and their resistance to change would be less. Whenever you evaluate resistance, try to determine the person's <u>readiness</u> to change, how prepared they are to change.

Finally, be aware if the person is <u>able</u> to make the changes you want them to make for you. For example, if you wanted a friend to baby-sit for you and he had a prior important engagement, he would no doubt resist you, perhaps becoming angry or stubborn. In any case, much energy would be expended resisting you.

Usually, the more difficult the change, the more resistance occurs. You may get many questions and perhaps accusations of your being selfish. People may also feel very anxious. People need their anger, frustration, resistance, or anxiety in order to make the change that you want them to make. Again, people resist change because they fear the outcome, which is unknown. However, once they transcend resistance and these feelings, they will feel happy. They will feel successful with you, especially when you <u>reward</u> them for making the change to please you. Always express appreciation.

Positive Acknowledgment

One way to help you get through another person's resistance is to give the person a positive acknowledgment. Use positive words to give the other person credit. This will influence their reaction to you and they will respond in a way that is more pleasing. Giving credit means you respect the person's opinion or viewpoint, even if you don't particularly like what they've said. The use of a positive acknowledgment is designed to help shift the person from being critical or judgmental to being more positive and accepting of you. It diminishes their need or desire to resist. Additionally, it disarms the other person, in a non-confrontational way, because they feel accepted by you. They feel heard and understood. They now have less of a need to be critical, judgmental, or aggressive with you.

Another aspect of positive acknowledgment is that it automatically puts you in the authoritative role in a way that is acceptable to the other person. Why? Because you take the initiative in determining what is good or acceptable about what they've said, and giving them credit for that - whether you agree or not. Using a positive acknowledgment can also be used very effectively with people who are already in a positive state of mind. It will further them to support your view point.

Use a positive acknowledgment statement primarily when someone is being critical or judgmental, which may make you feel uncomfortable. Positive acknowledgment statements can also be very effective when dealing with aggressive people. It helps defuse the person's (passive) anger with you, even if you've done something to hurt, frustrate or discomfort them. People will be more receptive and listen to what you are saying when you first use a positive acknowledgment. Further, it provides you with a lead in to using direct anger to tell the person what to do for you to make you happy or to feel more comfortable. This also makes it much easier for you to not take on the other person's problem.

In short, using a positive acknowledgment statement sets the tone for a <u>positive</u> conversation between yourself and the person. You invariably will have more success with people when you deal with them within a positive framework rather than a negative one. Then people will see you as being more confident, secure, decisive, and in control. These qualities all convey a sense of ease, security, and reassurance. People will like you more, respond to you better, and they will think that <u>you</u> like <u>them</u> more. Moreover, when you are in a positive position, people will feel freer to express their true viewpoint about things, reassured that they would not be criticized by you.

Let's look at some positive acknowledgment examples. If you are being criticized, judged, or verbally attacked by someone, use positive acknowledgment statements:

A. "Thank you for coming to me and helping me to understand the problem."
B. "I'm glad you are telling me how you feel."
C. "Thanks for taking the time to go over this with me."

People hearing these responses do not feel threatened or offended. They feel accepted. Again, you are in the authoritative role: telling others what is good or acceptable about what they are saying to you. Now you are in a position to start using direct anger to tell the person what to do for you.

For example, if a person says: "You made a mistake today! You were supposed to call before you came over here. You know I am not ready." What is that person's problem? They are concerned about being ready. This is the person's insecurity, not yours. This is an ideal time to use a positive acknowledgment statement. Your response: A. "Thanks for telling me that." B. "I appreciate your concern about my coming over." C. "I can see what you are saying about that." This sets up this conversation as more neutral and less confrontational. The person is upset with you, but you have neutralized the verbal attack on you. When most people accuse you of doing something to them, they automatically expect you to defend your position or attack back. Using the positive acknowledgment gives people a response they do not expect. You have given them credit and acceptance for what they have said. This, then, decreases their motivation to continue their verbal attack on you. All of these benefits make your life easier with that person, and they like you more as well.

Another way to reduce people's resistance: Be as clear as possible with the person about what you want them to do for you. The more they understand what you want them to do, the easier it will be for them to reduce their resistance. Use as much "positive selfishness" as you can. Think of yourself being a teacher who is providing all the necessary information a person's needs to be a success with you.

You might say: "Go to the movies with me next Saturday at 8:00 p.m. I would really like that." Don't say:

"Do you feel like going to the movies?" The first statement is clear and specific about what you want (positive selfishness)). You are telling the person what to do to make you happy. You have also given a specific date and time. The second statement, which is actually a question, is not really clear as to what you want the person to do to make you happy. One might assume that you want the person to go to the movies with you, but that is not clear. In reality, you may not really want to see a movie. Moreover, a question conveys a sense of indecisiveness or even apprehension. This may create anxiety in the other person, which can cause them to resist.

Continue this process of being as clear as you can about what you want, and express the importance the issue has to you. The person will eventually be able to "borrow your confidence." If they lack sufficient strength to overcome their own resistance, they will be able to use your strength, which arises from using "positive selfishness."

Often we assume that the other person knows what we want them to do for us. Never assume this. Seldom do others really know what you want exactly without you telling them. Even if they did, they'd do what you wanted in their way, not yours. And this might not please you. We've all heard statements such as: "Well, he should have known that I don't like that?" This happens all of the time. Assuming others should know forces them to either guess or go through a trial-and error process to give us what we want. This is too difficult and frustrating. People end up resisting and you end up not getting what you want. To avoid this, be as *clear* as you can about what you want. Then use positive acknowledgment statements to overcome resistance. Both parties will enjoy better communication and a happier relationship.

Tapping Into the Person's Desire To Please

A basic human drive common to all is to seek gratification: to be satisfied and get our needs met. People seek gratification in many ways, but one aspect is very important: The desire to be successful. Success makes people feel good. It gives pleasure and a certain sense of gratification.

We also like to be successful with others, which makes us feel important and empowered. It allows us to share in the happiness of the other person whom we have pleased successfully. A person's desire to be successful is the key, the core link to what we call "tapping into a person's desire to please."

The Desire To Please

This valuable concept has been extremely effective in helping people overcome resistance and in motivating others to do things for you. Specifically, "tapping into a person's desire to please" uses specific words designed to stimulate a person's innate desire and motivation to please others and be successful. It involves the use of words which convey to the person that they would please you, satisfy you, or make you happy doing what you want them to do. Phrases include:

o "I'd appreciate that."
o "That would make me happy."
o "I'd love you for that."
o "This is really important to me."
o "It would really make me feel good."

These phrases do 3 things: 1. let the other person know that what you want is <u>meaningful</u> to you. In turn, this helps the person to be more focused on what you are saying. 2. let the person know they will be rewarded, they will experience gratification. They know if they can do what you want and make you happy, they will be a success with you. Being successful with you will give them a sense of gratification. 3. give the person a sense of empowerment; they had the power to make someone happy.

<u>How To Implement This Process</u>

The first thing needed is to get the person's full attention by directing them to listen to you. Then, use direct anger. As clearly as possible, give the person instructions telling them exactly what to do for you. Immediately, you would "tap into the person's desire to please." You would convey to them how pleased, happy, and good you'd feel when they did what you want them to do.

"Win-Win" Combo

"Tapping into the desire to please" is especially effective when a person is resisting doing what you want. It helps to motivate them to overcome their resistance and please you. After you use a direct anger statement, add phrases such as: A. "I'd really appreciate that." B. "That would really make me feel good." C. "That would make me happy."

These statements all "tap into the person's desire to please." They awaken the motivation to please you, and to be a success with you. A sense of gratification follows, which all of us like to experience. Using this process will help you to get your needs met much more often. And others will feel a sense of accomplishment doing what you want them to do. This is a foolproof "win-win" combination. You get your needs met (positive selfishness) and the other person is rewarded -- (i.e., feeling a sense of empowerment by pleasing you and being rewarded for that.)

Use of Understanding

Everyone wants to be understood. This is a major emotional need, to feel understood. Invariably, we feel better when people understand us. And the more we feel understood, the more receptive we will be to another person's point of view.

How To Convey Understanding

Simply tell someone: "I understand what you are saying." This does not imply that you understand the *meaning* of what they are saying or that you agree or disagree with them. That is, you do not necessarily understand the substance of their words, but that you are *listening* to them. This acknowledgment helps the person to feel understood. Now they have less of a drive to press their point, their resistance, or any verbal attack of you. They are now in a much more receptive state of mind to *listen* to what you might have to say, switch to another issue, or be more *open* to do what you want them to do. Essentially, the use of understanding "disarms a person" and makes things easier for you.

You can also use understanding when someone is very emotional about a particular issue, in which you don't want to become involved. Your use of understanding in this situation, allows you to simply listen without becoming involved in their problem.

To help a person overcome their resistance or to reduce their pressure or verbal attack, you are not limited to: "I understand." Other phrases are equally effective. They include:

1. "You have a good point."
2. "I like what you just said."
3. "Thanks for telling me that."
4. "I'm happy that you said that."

Notice that in none of these phrases did you voice agreement with what they said. You only conveyed your understanding. You may not even like the other person's point, what they just said, or want to thank them for it. But using these type of phrases communicates to the person that you *understand them as people*. You are also conveying respect for them. Their feeling of being understood will reduce resistance, verbal attacks, and help others be *more open* to what you want them to do.

Free Will

"Free Will" is having the freedom to do what we want. This is a very important concept in using the "Lewis Approach." It is important to allow others to have their "free will."

"Free will" allows people the freedom to accept or reject what you say. In using positive selfishness, we always acknowledge the other person's "free will:" the right to do or not do what we want them to do. This must be their choice. God has given all of us "free will" - to either worship Him or not. This does not mean that you have to tell people that they have "free will." You simply accept their right to have "free will." This, in effect, removes pressure from the other person. Acceptance of their "free will" tends to help people be more open and objective in their decisions because pressure is decreased. However, you want to be as clear as possible when you tell people what to do for you.

140

Give them their "free will" but don't give them any other choices, or alternatives. You want to influence their "free will" but not control it. This might sound like a contradiction, but it is an important distinction. You focus only on what you want, clearly and specifically, while allowing the other person their "free will" to please you or not. They can either decide to do what you want or not, based on their ability to do so. If you give them alternative choices, they may choose something other than what you really want. Don't give people choices that you are not willing to accept.

Additionally, if you were to give a person a choice, they will usually choose <u>what they want you to have</u>, rather than what <u>you</u> really want. You only give them the choice to either <u>do or not do what you want them to do for you.</u> You don't give them choices as to <u>what</u> you want them to do for you. That is <u>your</u> choice only.

Summary: Give people the "free will" to decide if they can do what you want them to do for you. Focus only on telling the person concisely what to do for you, and its importance to you. This gives both parties control. You control what you want them to do, and they control whether to do so or not. Thus, you are in a better position to accept their choice. If they did not do what you wanted them to do, you'd be in a better position to know how to influence their decision, using one of the other tools in overcoming resistance. When you allow people the right to exercise their "free will," it becomes much easier for them to come through for you and make you happy.

The "3 Times Rule"

The "3 Times Rule" is another very effective way to overcome someone's resistance. Why do people resist? Often, they are focused on their own concerns and simply did not "hear" your message. Or if they did hear, they prefer to focus on their issues.

To overcome this type of resistance, use the "3 Times Rule." Tell the person what you want them to do for you up to three times. The first time, the person is focused on his or her own thoughts and either may not have heard you or it did not register. The second time, they may hear part of what you said, but it may only nominally register in their mind. The third time, use their name to get their full attention. Now, you have their attention; they have "heard" your message, and it is registered in their brain.

Remember, always tell them precisely what you want and to do that for you. The clearer and more detailed your instruction, the easier it will be for them to decide to do it for you.

Why the "3 Times Rule" works. Why do you use this? The first time we tell people to do something for us, and they don't, we feel rejected or upset. The "3 Times Rule" assures that your message has been heard. You will not feel rejected or disappointed simply because the person did not hear you. After you have used the "3 Times Rule", you know they have heard you. Now they may decide not to do what you want. Either they don't know <u>how</u> to do it, or they don't possess the power to do so.

An example of the "3 Times Rule" to overcome resistance effectively. You want a co-worker at your office to provide you with a business report. This person is upset about being over worked and feels no one cares about her. You know she is a resource and has the best ability to do this job. Say to the person: "Tell me when you can give me a summary of the business activity we had on the Jones account for last month?" Her response: "I'm not going to give a report. No one appreciates what I do around here." Obviously there is a problem. Use the "Three Times Rule." Tell the person: "I didn't know you felt that way. But, *work it out to give me the report.*" She replies: "Why should I do the report? Now one else does anything around here." Your response: "I understand how you feel and am glad you are sharing that with me. But, *arrange to give me that report this afternoon anyway* (second of the "3 Times Rule"). I'd really appreciate that." She says: "If I do this report, what am I going to get for this? Will I be appreciated more?" Your reply: "I understand what you are asking and you have a good point. But it is really important the report is done. So, *work it out to get the report in this afternoon.* I would really like that." After this third time, you can be sure she heard you. If she still resists, there must be something else getting in her way of doing it.

After the person comes through for you and does what you want, reward them with a "thank you" or otherwise express your appreciation. This creates a good feeling in the other person. It also helps you to dismiss any remnant guilt feelings you may have from using direct anger (i.e. instructional statements). The "3 Times Rule" works very well in overcoming resistance and enhancing clearer communication.

Subjective in An Objective Way

There is another concept effective in overcoming resistance: "Subjective in an Objective way." This means that you present your story (from your viewpoint, which is subjective) in an objective way. We are defining objective as dealing with facts or issues free of distortion by personal feelings or prejudices. You point out the facts which emphasize your point of view.

Being "subjective in an objective way" is an important concept. It allows the other person to better trust what you say and be more willing to do what you want. When you focus on getting what you want, you must be subjective, (i.e., be personal about what you want.) When you're subjective, you think only of your own needs. This is "positive selfishness" designed to make you happy, but not at the other person's expense. When you're being subjective, you are just clarifying what you want done for you.

At the same time, however, you must be objective about _how_ you present your subjective or personal view. You do this by transcending your personal emotions when you express your viewpoint. You present the facts of your personal viewpoint as objectively as you can. This helps influence the person to view the issue from _your_ perspective. This, in turn, helps reduce or eliminate the person's resistance towards you. When you present the facts objectively, others feel as if they have a choice to exercise their "free will." They don't feel forced or pressured. Further, people have a tendency to _appreciate_ your objectivity and non-pressuring behavior. Thus, they are more willing to listen to your viewpoint and be more receptive to you. However, keep in mind that the _substance_ of your message is not objective; it is subjective. Your goal is to influence the person toward your viewpoint without pressure or coercion.

Obviously, people generally resist when you _impose_ your views on them. That is being subjective in a _subjective_ way. This method dishonors the person's "free will," which disavows their right to make a decision based on your facts. Such imposition is negative selfishness, which creates defensiveness and resistance in others. This process makes it difficult, if not impossible, to get what you want. Being "subjective in an objective way" is the healthy alternative. This concept may sound unique and different, and it is. It is one of the best ways to overcome resistance.

To illustrate from a real life situation:

Peter is called to court to testify for a friend accused of stealing a case of beer. A bystander, who allegedly witnessed the criminal act, will also testify. One would assume the bystander's testimony would be more reliable and objective. However, if Peter testifies as to his friend's whereabouts during the crime and emphasizes his friend's honesty, one would give more weight to Peter's testimony. How could Peter's response on the witness stand be "subjective in an objective way?" Here's how:

Prosecuting Attorney: Did you see the accused drinking beer that night or hear him say that he had?

Peter: Well, I did see him that night and it is difficult to recall what precisely happened. My best memory is that he was not drinking nor did he mention that he was.

If Peter had said, "Absolutely not!" That would be less objective and harder to believe. Using "subjective in an objective way" makes Peter appear more believable.

Summary: In any situation, personal or professional, it is best to avoid being subjective in a subjective way. Being "subjective in an objective way" has positive advantages:

1. It is more effective in overcoming resistance.
2. It allows others to exercise their "free will" and make their own decisions.
3. It makes communication easier.

4. It is more effective in getting people to give you what you want.

Guilt Issues and How to Utilize

Whenever you express any anger, passive or direct, you automatically feel some guilt. With direct anger, however, guilt feelings are very minimal. With passive anger (i.e. criticizing, blaming, yelling, threatening, manipulating, questioning, forcing, or displaying physical violence) guilt feelings will be quite significant. Often people don't even realize they have this guilt. They simply feel awkward or upset.

Guilt, as defined here, is when a person feels they have done something wrong, bad, or have hurt or offended someone. Whether aware of it or not, guilt is automatic. When you express passive anger, guilt begins to weigh on you like a heavy burden.

Quite a few people have told us that they didn't believe they'd experience guilt if they did certain things. They thought if they expressed passive anger, they wouldn't feel any guilt. Invariably, they do experience some guilt.

Once you express passive anger, guilt has been created and essentially "sits" on your conscience. It begins to get heavier and heavier. When people feel this guilt, they begin to fight it. They actually start exerting "mental energy" to ward off the guilt. They may try to convince themselves they should not feel guilty, and then justify their behavior or words. All justifications and excuses, however, are a futile attempt to rid oneself of the guilt. Even if you're told you hurt a loved one's or a friend's feelings, you may try to convince yourself they deserved it. Eventually, you will end up apologizing, which is an attempt to be free of guilt feelings.

Unfortunately, your quality of life will have suffered, to some degree, because of the negative energy expended to try to ward off the guilt feelings.

The point is passive anger, justified or not, creates feelings of guilt, which you will have to confront and deal with. An easy way to recognize if you or another person feel guilty is by an attempt at justification. This is a dead giveaway! Another way to recognize guilt is when you or the other person apologizes.

Issues of guilt can play an important role when dealing with people to help them meet your needs. Awareness of guilt can help you overcome passive resistance. Passive resistance is manifested in sarcasm, passive aggression, rudeness, stubbornness, or simply resisting to intentionally hurt you. To reduce intentional resistance, tap into their existing guilt, which removes their need to resist. How do you tap into the person's guilt? Emphasize that they are hurting you or causing you confusion, discomfort, disappointment, etc.

You might say:

> A. "Oh no!" (said with emotion or frustration)
> B. "I knew you would say that." (said with disappointment or frustration)
> C. "Golly!" (said with discomfort or disappointment).

This taps into the person's guilt. This guilt already exists in that person's psyche; they know they have hurt you. They have used passive resistance, a type of passive anger, which automatically creates some guilt feelings.

"Tapping into guilt" reduces the person's need to hurt you as well as their need to resist. This process will make your life, as well as the other person's life, easier when dealing with people who are doing this with you because no one really wants to hurt another; it's just their attempt to get their needs met.

You can also use other phrases in addition to the above three "tapping into guilt" phrases. Any word or phrase which conveys to the person they are hurting you or causing you confusion, discomfort, disappointment, etc. can be used. That's the key. After you have overcome resistance and tapped into their guilt, give the person _credit_ for having given you what you wanted. Because of the benefits, we encourage you to "tap into a person's existing guilt" to help your life be easier and your relationships more harmonious.

Avoid "Guilt Trips"

When we first introduced our "tapping into guilt" concept to people, many mistook it as laying a "guilt trip" on someone. This is not what "tapping into guilt" is. There are distinct differences between these two. We teach "tapping into guilt" and discourage "guilt tripping." The key point of "tapping into existing guilt" is that the guilt is already there. Conversely, a "guilt trip" is to blame another in a critical way, or try to force others to feel guilty unjustly. This is an attempt to <u>manipulate</u> feelings or behavior. In effect, it is an attempt to "dump" a problem on someone else. You can recognize "guilt trips" by such phrases as:

A. "*You* don't care about me."
B. "*You* don't do anything for me anymore."
C. "*You* don't appreciate the things I do for you."

Those who try to lay a "guilt trip" on you are obviously feeling hurt or rejected but are too dependent to verbalize that. Or they may not even know themselves. They are trying to get their needs met, but are unable to convey to you what those needs are. These people have unmet and strong <u>dependency</u> needs.

To summarize with an analogy: "Tapping into existing guilt" is like trying to get oil out of a full well. (The oil is there, you are simply tapping into it.) "Guilt tripping" is like trying to get oil out of an empty ditch!

One method we use in the "guilt tripping" process is what we call, the "bullfight." Just as the matador deftly moves out of the bull's way as it charges, we too can protect ourselves from "charging bulls." Like the matador in a bullfight, protect yourself from being "charged" by people and weaken their verbal attack on you.

How to do this? Remember one of our first concepts: think of yourself as perfect as you are. This helps you to move out of the way of the "charging bull." If you <u>don't</u> think of yourself as perfect, you'd become defensive and try to prove the person wrong. If you do this, you will have been "guilt tripped" by the person and left yourself in the path of the "charging bull."

By seeing yourself as perfect as you are, you dodge the
bull's horns and stay out of the way of the person's
verbal attack.

The next step is to "tap into the person's existing
guilt." You express to the person that they have hurt or
caused you some type of pain or discomfort. This will
weaken the person's verbal attack on you (the matador
jabbing the bull in the neck). Just as the picadors weaken
the bull, guilt weakens the person's verbal attack. Then the
person will recognize the hurt caused you.

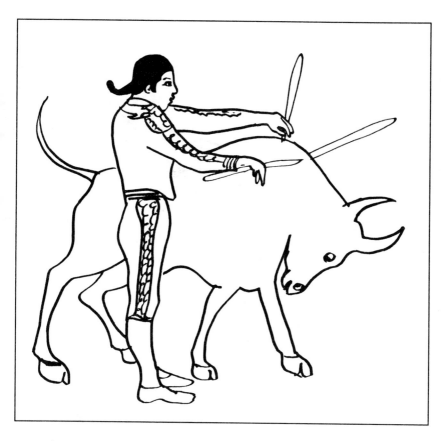

The Matador jabbing the bull with picadors represents your "tapping" into the person's existing guilt" as a result of them expressing passive anger toward you.

The next step is to use a positive acknowledgment statement. This gives others credit for their viewpoint which enables them to be more receptive to your point, which you convey using direct anger. In the bullfight, positive acknowledgment would represent the matador acknowledging the bull and its efforts.

The Matador acknowledges the bull for its efforts.
This represents you using a positive acknowledgment
statement.

Finally, use direct anger and tell the person what to
do for you (the matador directing the cape in front of the
bull). Using direct anger statements weakens the drive to
lay a "guilt trip" on you. You have, in effect, shifted the
focus of the conversation. When you operate from this

position, you cannot be "guilt tripped" because you are _taking charge_ of how the person will respond to you. What happens next is that the people become more aware of what they _really_ want. They then search for ways to tell you more clearly what that is, instead of trying to manipulate you.

An automatic benefit: This strengthens people's ability to communicate with you more directly, which makes things easier for you.

Here are several key phrases to help defuse "guilt trip" attempts on you:

1. "Oh, no!"
2. "There you go again!"
3. "You said it again!"
4. "I can't believe you said that!"

Summary: If someone tries to lay a "guilt trip" on you (blaming, criticizing, forcing you to feel guilty, etc.) when you have done nothing to justify it, first think of yourself as perfect as you are. This helps put you in the correct frame of mind. Then, "tap into the person's existing guilt" to protect yourself from verbal attacks or attempts at manipulation. Next, use a positive acknowledgment statement, which makes them more receptive to your point. Finally, use direct anger to instruct the person what to do for you (i.e., make their needs more clear as opposed to trying to lay a "guilt trip.") These four steps will keep you "on your feet" and away from being "guilt tripped."

Key Phrases To Use and Why

The Words and The Process

This section emphasizes the importance of the use of words as well as the process. Experience confirms that there is a <u>balance</u> between the use of the words <u>and</u> the process. However, you can use either. The process will work because it will lead you to the right words. But, if you are still learning the process, using the appropriate words will automatically drive the process for you. When you begin to use our approach, we strongly recommend that you memorize the proper words.

This chapter specifically gives you an effective working menu of words and "phrases" to use, plus guidelines as to when to use each of the selected phrases.

One important point: When you are learning the words, **say them exactly as written**. This is vital. If you don't, you could change the meaning as well as the process and not achieve the desired results. Resist this temptation to change the words. Read them verbatim and allow the process to work for you. This is taking responsibility for getting your needs met - positive selfishness.

Here's an example of how vitally important it is to *state the words as written*. "Call me tomorrow in the afternoon," a key phrase, is a direct anger statement. It gives clear direction, keeps you in control of what you want, and effectively prevents arguments. If you changed our key phrase to: 1. "Would you call me tomorrow?" 2. "It would be nice if you called me tomorrow." 3. "You never call me the way you used to.", (all passive anger statements), you will have changed the *meaning* of your intent and are less clear as to what you want others to do for you. More importantly, by changing the key phrase statement, you have lost control of your role in the conversation; you have left others free to interpret what you want. Their choice is theirs, not yours. Further, you have given them opportunity to make excuses as to why they didn't do what you wanted. Again, to get what *you* want, use our key phrase statements *verbatim*. We know from experience, this will give you success. People will do more things for you, you will feel better, and they will like you more. It is vital to stress, again, that you want to give others *your* choices of what you want them to do. This is an important point in using the key phases most effectively.

Simply tell them what to do for you without giving them any choices. Then they have the "free will" to do or not do what you want them to do for you. Remember, you are telling them exactly what to do for you. You are not polling them, seeking their opinion, or asking a question. This makes it as easy as possible for the person to understand what you want them to do for you, which increases the probability of your success with them.

<u>Key Phrases</u>

The following words and phrases can be used in any situation. Select and use these words to apply to your particular situation. Even when you master the process, you may sometimes become so upset you may have to consciously use these words again and again to avoid unpleasant or uncomfortable situations.

Most of the key phrase statements are either "direct anger" or "instructions." Each set of key phrases is grouped, titled, and geared to common situations. These statements also automatically keep you in charge of your involvement in the conversation.

A. <u>When you want to change the thinking, actions, demands or request of you by another person:</u>

- **<u>Be nicer to me</u>.** This first allows the person to know, without being threatened or challenged, that they are <u>not</u> being nice to you. It does not threaten the person because <u>you</u> are taking responsibility for defining what you need. You have clearly stated what you want. They can do it or not. The key point is that you made it <u>easier</u> for the person to know what to do for you: be nicer.

- **<u>Change the way you think about it.</u>** This conveys that their choice is different from yours and that you want them to do something that is more comfortable for you. This is clear information in a non-threatening manner. It also directs the person to consider your feelings without threatening them.

- **Make it easier for me**. This implies that what the other person is asking is difficult for you to do. Again, non-threatening and non-challenging. It conveys your willingness to go along with them but that their request is greater than what you are able to do.

- **Give me more choices**. You are not comfortable with the choices given you and also tells the person that what they want from you may be too much. This phrase can also be used to help the other person "think through" what they really want. The person may be asking or demanding things of you that would not help them or, even worse, could hurt them or yourself. This instruction will help the person to _really_ think about what they want of you before they make demands. This clear and non-challenging statement is easy to understand.

- **Don't ask me to do that**. Used when a person asks you something you _really_ don't want to do or cannot do, yet you want to be supportive. Again, this does not threaten or reject the person. This phrase also alerts others to the fact that what they are asking you may hurt themselves, you, or another person or object.

- **Ask me to do something else**. Best used when someone makes an unrealistic request for you. Tell them to ask you to do something else as many as three times. This also helps a person to be more creative or realistic and think of something else for you to do. This phrase can help them to give you other choices that you'd be more receptive.

- **Stop doing (or saying) that.** An acceptable way to change the person's aggression towards you. You are telling them clearly, in a non-confrontational way, you do not like what they are doing or saying. You make it clear to the other person what you want them to stop doing or saying and it calls for prompt action on their part.

- **Change what you are doing (or saying).** Best used when a person insults or criticizes you. It leaves the choice up to the other person, but conveys that what they are doing or saying hurts or bothers you. Nobody really wants to hurt another person. They only want is to get their needs met. Again, this phrase does not confront or challenge, nor put the person on the defensive. It allows the person to find alternatives to try to get their needs met.

- **Ask me to do something that I can do.** This phrase can be used when asked to do something beyond your physical, emotional, or spiritual ability. The person's request may be unrealistic. Sometimes people set you up to do something that they know you cannot do. When you refuse, an argument could ensue. This phrase clearly conveys that you cannot do what they ask and puts the burden of their request back on them. However, you are not rejecting them or "blocking their progress" in terms of what they want from you.

- **<u>Stop pressuring me</u>.** Especially effective when someone is very upset and makes demands of you. You may resist only because of their pressure. You help the person see what they are doing to you. The person does not feel as though they are being judged by you. With this particular phrase, it is vital that you only use one anger at a time, direct. You may be in a highly emotionally charged situation. Don't say, "Stop pressuring me!!!" (with emphasis). Say it _without emphasis_ (i.e., one anger at a time, direct) and use a normal speaking tone, "Stop pressuring me" (no voice emphasis).

Use these key phrase statements when you want to protect or prevent yourself from being burdened by another person's request of you. All of these phrases will make things easier for you. Most importantly, none of them will challenge or threaten the other person so they will feel safe to listen to you. And you will be in a much better position to have your needs met in a non-confrontational atmosphere.

B. "Neutralizing/Transition" Phrases (similar to "Understanding / Positive Acknowledgment Statements): To keep yourself from involvement into a stressful verbal situation or conversation

(Note: After you use these phrases, follow with direct anger: telling the person what to do for you).

- **Let me think about that.** This phrase postpones your taking action on a request or question posed by another. It also makes it easy for the person to accept your switching to another point of view without their feeling neglected or rejected. Perhaps most importantly, it conveys to the person that you have *heard* what they have said and are working on responding. It precludes a potential verbal attack on you and allows you to get to your issue.

- **That's a good point. But, let me share something with you.** This phrase indicates that you have heard their viewpoint, while it diminishes the intensity of their verbal attack or pressure on you. Then you guide them to focus on your viewpoint. After you use this key phrase and tell them your viewpoint, use direct anger and tell them what to do for you.

- **Let me come back to that point later. (Then continue with your point).** Again, this phrase acknowledges what the person said and directs them to postpone talking about their issue. It also provides you a "transition" from their topic to your topic, without any negative feelings generated.

- **I considered that you might raise that particular question. Let me say it this way.** This phrase conveys the fact that you were thinking of them or their point of view. This encourages and motivates them to _pay attention_ to what you have to say and, thus, be more likely to comply.

- **That's a good question. (idea, statement, etc.) Let me respond to that this way.** (then tell them what **you want them to know**) This phrase makes it clear that you are diverting or redirecting their statements or questions to _your_ idea and subsequent message. This helps motivate people to listen to you more objectively. Even though you have shifted the focus of the conversation, this phrase allows you to do so in a way that the person does not feel ignored, criticized, or unheard.

- **I was trying to figure that out myself (or I was thinking about that myself).** Extremely effective when being questioned about what you have done or been involved with, especially with others. This allows the person to participate in a positive and productive way. You also appear more responsible because you are trying to figure out the problem and work it through.

- **Thanks for telling me that. Let me consider that.** Here you are supportive of their viewpoint, which encourages them to be more supportive of your viewpoint. It also let's them know that you have heard what they have said, which makes them more receptive. Lastly, it does not criticize the other person so they will have little desire to challenge you.

- **I'm glad you brought that up. Thanks for doing that. But this issue is really important to me so go along with my way of seeing it.** (then tell them) This phrase is very effective with someone who has a viewpoint different from yours and strong feelings about it. It provides you a solid avenue to transition to your viewpoint. Then, thank them, which helps to neutralize their position (i.e., reduce the intensity of their viewpoint). Notice that you have not criticized or rejected them. This reduces their need to challenge you. Finally, you help them see the importance that your viewpoint has to you by using direct anger.

These key phrase statements work well in neutralizing and transitioning with people to avoid hassles. They also take the pressure off you, without placing any on the other person, and automatically helps to motivate the other person *to do what you want them to do for you.*

C. When you want the other person to do something for you

- **Let me have it my way.** Instead of putting another on the defensive, this gives the person the option to do, or not do, what you want them to do. It clearly conveys what you want. If they decide to go along with you, they will do so because they want to, that it would be pleasing them (i.e. they'd want to please you).

- **Agree with me and support my idea.** This non-pressure phrase guides other to agree with you. The choice is theirs, but phrased for the person to agree with you, because it is a direct anger statement. The other person can see that agreeing with you would support you, make you happy, and that <u>they</u> are important to you. This will increase their desire and motivation to do what you want them to do and like you more in the process.

- **Go out of your way for me and .... (tell them to do for you).** This clear statement makes it easier for the person to decide because it gives the direction that you want them to go. They understand that if they do what you want them to do, they will please you. This phrase is also very effective in reducing resistance.

- **<u>Don't think of what you want, think only of what I want and...... (tell them what to do for you)</u>**. A more assertive statement without pressure. You simply give directions. This leaves room for the person to tell you what <u>they</u> think in a sharing spirit. It also conveys the importance that the issue has to you. This key phrase freely leaves the choice to the person to do what you want them to do.

- **<u>Change the way you see it and see it my way</u>**. With respect, you tell them to make a change for you. It allows the person to understand that you want it your way, but not at their expense. This phrase reduces the possibility of resistance. Note that when the person decides to change for you, it's their own decision based on their desire to please you.

- **<u>Do it my way. Do such and such..... (What you want them to do for you)</u>**. This let's the person know that you want it your way, without them having to think about what to do. When you use this phrase, you will find that unless the other person has some strong objections to doing what you want them to do, they will do it your way *and feel good about it*. This also applies to people who don't like you or want you to have your way. (This may sound unlikely, but it is true. We have seen this often and again throughout the years).

- <u>Talk to me the way I want you to talk to me. Tell me.... (Tell them talk nicer to you, be more respectful, more understanding, etc.</u>) This phrase does not tell the person to stop talking to you *their* way, which would be criticism. Instead, it tells them *how to talk to you* in a way that pleases you.

- <u>Arrange to go with me this afternoon.</u> This phrase tells the person to do something for or with you. It is their option to say yes or no, after you clarify what you want. You are not trying to force or manipulate. You tell the person to do things that please you. If they have no strong objections, they will decide to go along with you.

- <u>Work it out so that I can have it my way (Then tell them what to do for you).</u> You give the person the "assignment" of doing something to please you. When you tell them how to work it out, your way, they feel empowered. This is non-confrontational, devoid of pressure or criticism. It simply gives them a successful "assignment" to do for you.

- <u>Listen to me and hear what I'm telling you. Then, tell me what you understand.</u> Use this phrase when you feel someone is either not listening or misinterpreting what you are saying. This phrase helps the person so that they can listen to you and hear what you have to say. Effective when dealing with those who are very anxious, nervous, or emotionally upset. It provides the structure the person needs, to listen, focus, and control their emotions.

These key phrase statements are very effective. Use these clear instructional statements (direct anger) to get what you want, the right words for the appropriate situation. They work! You will be happy and others will feel successful doing things for you!

D. **"Tapping Into Guilt": How to utilize guilt in a person to reduce their resistance or protect yourself from their passive anger.**
(Note: These phrases and words are most effective when said with strong emotion which expresses disgust or disappointment.)

- **Oh No!** Used after a person expresses passive anger toward you, to reduce the intensity of their passive anger. The person then begins to explain himself or herself. Follow with an instruction (direct anger). If the person continues to express passive anger, repeat the phrase, "Oh No!" or a similar one. Again, look for an explanation and a decrease in their aggression towards you. This phrase can be used as many as three times.

- **That's not fair!** (said with emotion) This phrase is used when a person expresses passive anger towards you or excludes you from something. Use this phrase as many as three times. It helps them to see the negative impact of their words. They will begin to explain or justify their action. This phrase will also reveal their own guilt feelings. Follow this up quickly with an instruction (direct anger).

- **I knew you would say that.** (said with emotion) Used in a similar situation, as above.

- **That hurts.** (said with emotion) People who express passive anger are not trying to hurt you, but only trying to get their needs met. When they realize your feelings are hurt, they will change. Follow up with an instruction (direct anger). If they can include your instruction with their getting their needs met, they will. This allows others to feel the guilt of their passive anger and to have information for making their decision.

- **Not that.** (said with emotion) This phrase focuses on a particular subject, but conveys that what the person is saying is distressing to you. Again, follow this phrase with an instruction. The person will adjust what they are saying and reduce their passive anger towards you.

- **Golly!** (with emphasis and irritation) This protest makes the person think of what they are saying and how they are saying it. Used to utilize guilt or even to help make the person happy for doing something good for you. A versatile phrase.

- **There you go again.** (said with emphasis) This phrase can be used very effectively to increase the other person's guilt level. After the person begins to explain, you take charge of your role in the conversation simply by giving an instruction statement (direct anger). After the person is finished explaining, again use an instruction statement (direct anger) to guide the person to do what you want him or her to do.

- **I can't believe you said that.** (said with emphasis) This conveys very strongly that the person has said something that you do not like or which has hurt you.

- **Stop hurting my feelings.** (said with emotional feeling) Directly tells the person that they are hurting you. Again you can use this up to three times, but <u>not</u> in a row. Wait for a response before you say it again.

- **Oh, that's what you think.** (emphasize the word "that's") It conveys that you have discovered how others are trying to fool you, whether they really are or not, and that you do not like what they said. If needed, repeat this up to three times. It makes others aware of their internal intentions.

All of the above key phrase statements will work well when you want to utilize guilt in others to reduce their resistance or protect yourself from their passive anger. Be aware also of how others begin to explain themselves and, then, how their passive anger diminishes. This is the key. You will know you have used the key phrase correctly when you see this happening. At this point, you are in a comfortable position to tell them what to do for you - and they will be in a better frame of mind to respond positively.

Chapter 7

How To Know You Got What You Wanted

Often we have noticed that people who use our approach will get what they want, but not recognize that. This may sound strange, even somewhat unbelievable, but it is true. In order to know that you got what you wanted, you must <u>first</u> know what it is that you want from the other person. A very simple example: If you wanted a glass of water, told the person to bring you that, and they complied, then you got what you wanted. This is obvious. Everyone would recognize that.

However, in other situations, people <u>think</u> that they know what they want, but they don't. They may have an idea, but may not be sure. This uncertainty is also present in people with whom you are dealing. For example, a friend invites you to their house to watch a special on TV. When you arrive, no one is home. The next time you see this person, what do you want from him or her. An apology? A gift to compensate? Nothing? Only you can know exactly what you want.

Know What You Want

Specifically and in detail, it is important to know what you want. If you are not sure, guess. Be actively involved in directing the person to give you what you want. Do not assume or let the other person try to figure out what _you_ want. Be as specific as possible in communicating to the person _what you want and how they can give you what you want_. The more specific and detailed, the better and the easier it will be for the person to please you. Focus on telling the person the specific action you want taken. The better they understand this, the more willing people will be to do what you want. They may want to please you, but may be afraid to take the risk, unless you fully clarify your needs. People will be hesitant for fear of failure.

None of us really want to hurt others. Sometimes, however, the only way others know how to attempt to get what they want and get their needs met is to attack verbally. Most of us succumb to this. Again, this relates to dependency. We may not even "feel" the dependency.

How to best avoid this? _Know_ precisely what you want from other people, believe that you _will get_ what you want, and then help the other person _understand_ how to give you what you want.

172

Sometimes we get what we want, but not exactly <u>when</u> we want it. Sometimes we partially get what we want, but not all at the same time. Recognizing that you got what you wanted only partially will help you determine what is preventing the person from giving you the balance of what you want. When you know the obstacles, you can then help others to remove them (i.e., resistance, barriers, etc.). Other times you may get what you want, but it is mixed with things that you don't want. Recognize those things that you wanted and leave the rest alone.

It is important to know that you got what you wanted so you will be more satisfied in your relationships. You will get what you want more often because of this ability to recognize that you got what you wanted. Conversely, if you fail to recognize this, you might try to change or force the other person and, thus, meet with resistance and resentment, which creates more difficulty. In essence you'd still be trying to tell others what to do for you and they would have already given you what you wanted. When you've gotten what you wanted, remember to thank or reward the person. And the issue is over.

But if you fail to recognize that you got what you wanted, you may become involved in an argument or an unpleasant conversation. In order to fully recognize that you did get what you wanted, be clear, in your own mind, as to exactly what your needs are. Of course, what you want originally may change at any given point, as other information presents itself. So, be aware and take full responsibility for knowing what you want and using the "Lewis Approach" to achieve your goals.

Let's look at an example: Judy wanted her boyfriend to visit her at her house, but he was very busy with a new assignment. Finally, he arranged to see her, but when he got there, he became critical. Judy got what she wanted: her boyfriend came to see her. She could have been upset about his being critical of her. But, Judy recognized she got what she wanted and told him that she was happy that he had visited. Once she did that, he stopped criticizing her and they had a good visit together. However, had he continued to criticize her, she would have told him to be nicer and say good things about her. As he attempted to do this for her, she'd focus on the positive words he used to give her what she wanted. She'd acknowledge and give him credit for doing that.

To determine if you got what you wanted, you have to clearly know what you wanted and if you got it. You also <u>listen</u> to the other person's words to see if they are saying what you wanted them to say. Acknowledge and recognize all of the positives, or all parts of the person's statement that you like. If parts are negative, focus on the positives and acknowledge this to the other person.

In their attempt to give you what you want, many people fear that they will fail you and be criticized. Therefore, they will either resist giving you what you want, or only give you partially what you want in order to feel safe. This is important. People should feel safe with you.

Again, recognize this so you don't feel frustrated, believing you did not get anything. Recognize that you did get part of your needs met. You can then continue to instruct them further. One phrase might be: "I understand that I may want more, but it is important to me that you are pleasant to me. So say nice things to me to make me feel good." Then, listen to the other person's words. You might hear this question: "Why should I be nice to you?" Or, "Are you nice to me?"

Recognize that you are getting closer to what you want. Instead of answering the question, tell the person that you understand what they are saying and continue to instruct the person to give you what you want. Say: "I understand what you asked me. But be pleasant to me. It is important that you do this for me." Again, listen to the other person's reply. It may be another question. They might say: "What do you want me to say to you?" This shows that the person's resistance is almost gone, and they are now in a frame of mind to consider what you want them to do. One important point: when you instruct someone to give you what you want with words, _avoid_ answering questions. Instead, give an instruction (i.e., direct anger). For example: "I am glad you asked that. _Tell me that you like me and that you are happy to be with me._"

You did not answer the question, but you did acknowledge it. The instruction helps the person to overcome their last resistance to give you what you want. At this point, the person might reply: "I am happy to be with you, I do care about you, and I want you to be happy." Listen to these words. Have you now gotten what you wanted? You sure did! At this point you would reward the person for giving you what you wanted: "Thanks for telling me that. It really makes me feel good."

Summary: When you hear a positive, even if mixed with a negative, it indicates you got what you wanted, at least partially. Recognize and acknowledge this. Thank and/or compliment the person for the part that you liked. This rewards and automatically motivates them to _continue_ to give you what you want. And you help them find ways to give you more of what you want. It also reinforces in your own mind that you got what you wanted. This is very important. As you continue to focus on the positives, the negatives will eventually vanish, and you will get more fully what you really wanted - and more often.

Chapter 8

Getting Out Of Trouble - "The Life Raft"

This chapter focuses on how to fully utilize the "Lewis Approach" to avoid feeling discomfort or any residue of anger. If you do feel anger building up inside, then you are not fully using our approach or the exact words as outlined. If so, we want you to "get back to the life raft" and get yourself out of trouble. To get "back on track," use the "Lewis Approach." Let's see how this works.

You are engaged in an ordinary conversation. This represents being on a "life raft" in the middle of the ocean. But you find yourself disagreeing with or objecting to what the person is saying. You react using passive anger, instead of direct anger. Now you feel upset, (i.e., you are off the "life raft" and into the cold ocean). Use more passive anger and your rage increases. Now, in fact, you are beginning to drown in the middle of the cold dark ocean. Stop! Here is where you pull out our book and begin to swim back to your "life raft."

"Life Raft" Concept

The origin of this concept is interesting. One of the clients that Chuck Lewis had worked with said he knew how to apply some of our approach in practice (in a live conversation), but sometimes failed to get the expected results. As we listened, we realized the man was simply too upset and had left out key parts of our approach. Passive anger precluded him from being effective with others. This caused him to fall off the "life raft."

To effectively use our approach, you must adhere to its key principles. Some of the principles typically not followed include:

a. becoming dependent by wanting the other person to try to figure out what you want (i.e., not using enough positive selfishness).
b. trying to take away the other person's free will by making or forcing the them to do something.
c. using more than one anger at a time.

All of these things can get you into trouble and block your effectiveness in getting the results you want. Be sure you are fully and completely using all components of our approach. The results will not disappoint you.

However, we realize this may not always be possible. We are all human. Despite our understanding and best efforts, we sometimes become upset or even very angry (i.e., give in to our feelings of dependency). When this happens, we will most probably resort to our old, ineffective ways of dealing with problems. When we fall back into this mental state of dependency, we find that situations become worse, not better, and could get out of hand: arguments, verbal battles, conflicts, etc. To avoid uncomfortable situations, use the "Lewis Approach," follow the principles, and stick with them!

If you do slip back and get into trouble, what can you do? You would "swim to the life raft" and get back on track (i.e., getting what you want). To swim back to the "life raft," do the following:

1. **Want things your way (Positive Selfishness).**
   Focus exclusively and only on what you want and think nothing of what the other person wants. Let others be free to think of what they want on their own. This avoids taking on someone else's problem. Say: "Instead of talking about what you want, focus on giving me everything I want. I'd appreciate that."

2. **Use Direct Anger by giving the person instructions as to what to do for you.**
   Direct anger is the most powerful form of anger you can use. It is the "Art of Using Anger without Being Angry." In fact, the person will feel that you really care about them! If they resist, tell them that you understand, as

a transition from their point to yours; then use more direct anger to tell them what to do for you. Be comforted in knowing that you are using the power of direct anger, which is tremendously effective.

3. **Think of yourself as being perfect the way you are.** This will prevent you from unnecessarily trying to correct yourself (which people have a tendency to do, which gets them off track and frustrated). Allow yourself to stay focused on your goal; what you want. It also keeps you from being manipulated. Think of the other person also as perfect for the same reasons. Focusing on your goal will automatically help others to correct themselves and avoid the other person's resistance.

4. **Allow others to have their "free will".** Continue, however, to pursue your goal; but don't try to control, manipulate, or force others. To do this robs them of their "free will". Focus on telling others what to choose (what you want), but allow them their "free will" and their ability to choose. This is the best path to success.

To get out of trouble, get back to the "Life Raft."

Whenever you find yourself getting angry in a passive way (i.e., blood pressure rising, feeling irritated, yelling, threatening, etc.), get back on the "life raft" via the four aspects outlined above. We are confident this will help you to get "back on track" to use the process effectively and successfully, which will definitely help you to enjoy your life more!

Chapter 9

Troubleshooting

Based on the experience and success we have had over the years in using the "Lewis Approach," we firmly believe our approach is as "foolproof" as anything can be. It has worked all of the time for us, in countless situations and varied circumstances. However in some situations, especially ones that involve the "8 Feet Rule," it may seem that this is not working. However, the only way it will not work is if you do <u>not</u> use it!

If you find yourself not getting results (as we have outlined), you may not be doing one of several things. One of these is that people instinctively try to *change other people*. Again, our approach is not designed to change people or force them to do anything they really do not want to do. The fact is, *you cannot change people*!

Our approach focuses only on getting people to do things for you <u>and</u> like it. As discussed throughout this book, what you are basically doing is instructing and **empowering** them to do what you want them to do for you.

If you think you are using our approach, but are not getting the results you want and are upset, you are not using our approach. It really does work all the time. Use the list below to "troubleshoot" and find where your breakdown is. Ask yourself:

1. Are you clear on your goals? (Knowing what you want as opposed to what you don't want).
(Solution: <u>Know</u> what you want).

2. Are you selfish enough?
(Solution: Be more selfish. Focus only on your needs).

3. Are you in control of presenting your problem or issue to the other person?
(Solution: Be in control of your problem or issue. Be <u>clear</u> about what it is you want).

4. Are you using more than one anger at a time?
(Solution: Use one anger (direct) at a time).

5. Are you asking or answering questions?
(Solution: Don't ask or answer questions).

6. Are you seeing yourself perfect as you are, and seeing others likewise as perfect?
(Solution: See yourself and others as perfect).

7. Are you instructing others well enough as to how to give you what you want?
(Solution: Be specific and instruct others as clearly as possible).

8. Are you trying to coerce or force others to do what you want them to do (i.e. thus trying to take away their "free will")?
(Solution: Don't try to force people to do things. Allow them their "free will").

9. Are you dependent on others?
(Solution: Be independent. Avoid being dependent on what others say, what they think, what their opinion is, etc. Tell them what to do, say, etc., for you).

10. Are you willing or ready to assume responsibility for the outcome of what you want?
(Solution: Take full responsibility for what you want).

Use what the solution says for each of the troubleshooting points listed above. This will really help you to stay on track and use our approach properly and effectively. And as a result, you will enjoy your life better and more fully.

Chapter 10

Getting What You Want: The "Lewis Approach"

This is the most significant part of this book, the "nuts and bolts" of how to use the "Lewis Approach." This chapter shows the entire process, from start to finish, on how you get what you want. Look at it as if it were the "Ten Commandments" of this book. As best you can, commit this process to memory. When you learn the process, it will expand your creativity to use various words and phrases to continue the process. Remember, getting what you want is a process; however, if you don't know the process, the words will drive the process for you.

Direct Anger is Empowering

Keep in mind that the crux of this entire process is knowing what anger (as specifically defined in this book) is and how it works, both for you and other person - the "Art of Using Anger Without Being Angry." Anger is the driving force behind everything. When you use direct anger properly, this process will work for you <u>every</u> time, <u>all</u> the time, as it has done for us throughout the years. Direct anger uses selected words to facilitate getting what you want <u>without imposing on other people</u>. This gives you the best possible chance to have them do what you want them to do for you. They will feel successful because they will have pleased you.

The process is comprehensive. But in at least 90 percent of the situations, you need not go past step six before you will have gotten what you wanted. When you do get what you want, <u>stop</u> the rest of the process. However, reward the person for giving you what you wanted. Use this process like a "light switch:" Turn it on only when you need it. Above all, stick with the process. It works! Have faith in this process, as well as in yourself. We guarantee that you will have fewer problems with people, begin to enjoy life more, like people more, and notice how people like you and do more for you.

The Process of the "Lewis Approach"

"Ground Rules"

A. <u>See yourself as perfect the way you are. Use Positive Selfishness (i.e. want everything your way). Express this by using direct anger.</u> Seeing yourself as perfect keeps you focused on the issue (what you want) as opposed to questioning yourself or evaluating what you want. It also reduces any feelings of guilt you may have as a result of using direct anger.

Using Positive Selfishness (i.e. wanting everything your way) allows the person to realize how important they are to you and <u>empowers</u> them to please. This also keeps the conversation riveted on the issue only: getting what you want.

B. <u>Don't try to force someone to change. Allow them to keep their "free will".</u> Only give them the option to do what you want them to do, the choice is theirs. Focus on what you want, <u>not</u> the person from whom you want it. This avoids falling into the trap of trying to force people to do things for you. If you try to take away someone's "free will," they will invariably resist.

C. <u>Don't try to get someone to do something for you at their expense.</u> Only have them do things that they are able to do, based on what they are telling you and how strongly they respond (i.e., look for "8 Feet"). If you try to get someone to do something at their expense, it will cause them to resist you - which makes getting what you want that more difficult.

D. <u>Don't ask or answer any questions.</u> This keeps you from being manipulated and allows you to stay <u>focused</u> and in <u>charge</u> of your issue. If you ask or answer questions, you change the topic and confuse the issue, which makes it harder for you to get what you want.

E. <u>Don't take on the other persons problem (i.e. don't try to tell the person how to solve their problem.)</u> If you take on a person's problem, you will be distracted from working on your own, or you would have a problem (the other person's) that you didn't have before. <u>Focus on your own issues and agenda and respond to those only.</u>

<u>Comprehensive Steps</u>

1. <u>Decide what you want.</u> Using Direct Anger, be direct and specific in telling the person <u>what to do for you.</u> Allow them to have the "free will" to try to please you.

If someone is criticizing, insulting or verbally attacking you, utilize "HTE" - "Have Them Explain." "Tell me why you are saying that." "HTE" is particularly effective when you feel a person is offending you.

2. <u>After using Direct Anger, expect them to resist.</u> Their resisting is healthy and necessary to help the person adjust to give you what you want.

3. <u>Be understanding of the person and indicate this.</u> The point is not necessarily understanding the meaning of what the person says but understanding their words. You tell the person that you understand what they are saying. This will help the person be more receptive to hear what you have to say.

4. <u>Tell them what to do for you, up to three times. ("The 3 Times Rule") using direct anger.</u> If they resist the first time, tell them that you understand them and then tell them what to do for you again. If they resist again, tell them to do it for you anyway and *stress the importance that the issue has to you.* If they are still resisting, move to step 5 below.

5. <u>Consider "8 Feet."</u> If they are still not doing what you want, there must be some barrier. Using direct anger, have them tell you what is getting in their way. This is "lowering the bar" for them to clear. You cannot be a source of their problem so don't accept that, even if you are. Look for something else. If people claim that you are the problem, you are being manipulated. If they say they are resisting because of you, tell them to give you other reasons.

6. Use "Neutralizing/Transition" phrases
(similar to "Understanding / Positive Acknowledgment"
statements). After the person responds by explaining
what is in their way, (which represents their attempt to
clear the "8 Feet" for you), if you still want them to do
something for you, use the Neutralizing/Transition
phrases: "Let me think about that.," "That's a good
point. Let me share something with you.," etc.

7. Use more Direct Anger/ Instructions. Immediately
following number 6 above, use more direct anger by
instructing the person to move the obstacle out of
their way. Help them to understand *the importance the
issue has to you* (i.e., *tap into their desire to please.*) This
empowers them (gives them your strength) to clear "8
Feet." This makes it easier for them to please you
because you gave clear instruction (via direct anger).

8. Utilize existing guilt. If the person at this point has not
done what you want them to do for you, two things
may be going on. First, the person may not have the
strength or ability to do what you want them to do.
Notice if they use a lot of "I" words and virtually no
"You" words. Do not try to force them to do what they
cannot do. This creates resentment. On the other hand,
if the person asks a lot of questions and uses lots of
"You" words, and virtually no "I" words, then the
person is probably just being stubborn. This
stubbornness represent "passive aggression" and
automatically creates a feeling of guilt in the person for
intentionally reacting as they have. Utilize this

existing guilt by helping the person see that what they are doing is hurting you.

9. <u>Be selfish (positively) and use more direct anger.</u> Immediately following step number 8 above, be more selfish (positively) by using more direct anger to help the person overcome their resistance. Be clear and specific about what you want them to do for you, focusing only on what you want.

10. <u>Use Rewards & Thank You's.</u> If the person comes through for you and does what you want them to do, reward them. Tell them you appreciate what they did for you, that it really made you feel good, really meant a lot to you, etc. This is important. Firstly, it helps you to acknowledge that you got what you wanted. Secondly, it reduces the natural feelings of guilt that you will have as a result of using the anger (direct) to get what you wanted. Furthermore, this keeps you from getting back into the issue and undoing the success that you have just had.

10A. If 10. did not happen (rare, if you are using our approach) and you still have not gotten what you wanted, the person may not have the ability to do what you want them to do for you, at least not at that particular time. It may be that what you want can be done more easily by another person. Or you may decide to get something else from that person. You may also find that later the person will have found a way to do what you want them to do for you. Before you leave the person, relieve yourself of the remaining guilt you will have as a result of using direct anger. Do this by thanking (rewarding) the person for discussing the situation or issue with you.

The "Lewis Approach," used as we have described in the above process, gives you the absolute best possible chance of getting what you want.

So, there is the process in its entirety: ten comprehensive steps. Learn them, memorize them, and, most importantly, <u>internalize</u> this process. You will discover that people are going out of their way to please you, you will feel better about yourself, and you will find that people like you more.

The Four-Step Process

When you are new to the process and still learning it, it may be difficult to remember each step in sequence and when to use each one. You may also find it challenging to remember the appropriate words to use when you are involved in a situation. To help you, we have designed and created the Four-Step process. This set of four different steps essentially encompass the ten comprehensive steps of the process, to a certain degree. When you are new at using the process, simply use the Four-Step process to get results quickly and easily.

The Four Steps:

1. Want everything your way. Tell people what or how to do for you.
2. Tell the person that you <u>understand</u> what they are telling you.
3. Tell them to be nice to you.
4. Don't ask and don't answer questions.

Step one of this four-step process is the primary one: It a. contains the action words, or direct anger; b. keeps you focused on your issue; c. and instructs people on how to please you. Steps two through four tie into step one.

Step two is used when someone resists you; you tell the person that you understand what they are saying. This will reduce their drive to resist and encourage them to be more open to what you want them to do. Then, immediately use step one again.

Step three is used if a person uses passive anger to verbally attack, criticize, judge, etc. <u>Tell them to be nicer to you</u>. You may not think something this simple works, but it does! We have used it countless times with excellent results. It's so simple that sometimes people are taken aback when you use step three. But then they get a good feeling about you; and they don't feel threatened or criticized. Further, step three helps awaken people's natural feelings of guilt which arise when they verbally attack you with passive anger. Essentially, this step slows down the verbal attack and offers a better platform to do what you want them to do for you. As with step two, after using step three, immediately follow up with step one again.

Lastly, step four, do not answer (or ask) questions! Questions are a set up to get you off track of your topic and manipulate you. More questions will follow. Instead, use step two and then immediately use step one again.

Summary: In a "nutshell,"

* Decide what you want and then use step 1.
* If they resist, use step 2, then step 1.
* If they criticize or attack you verbally, use step 3, then step 1.
* If they ask you questions, use step 4, then step 2, then step 1.

Follow these steps in this simple manner and you will find yourself using the "Lewis Approach" successfully and getting results!

NO

Don't force it! Don't use "Passive Anger," try to control, or take away
the person's "free will" to get them to do what you want.

YES

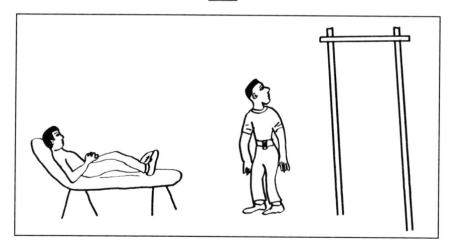

Easy does it! Use "Direct Anger," "Positive Acknowledgment," "Tap
Into The Person's Desire To Please," and "Utilize Guilt" to empower
the person to jump "8 Feet" and give you what you want.

Chapter 11

Getting What You Want - Detailed Examples

This chapter gives you a "front row seat" in using the "Lewis Approach" in a variety of real-life situations. This book gives you "real tools" and an approach that you can use in any situation to get positive results. Our approach empowers you and gives you a virtual "foolproof" way to get what you want. It has been used successfully in countless situations for over 25 years.

Of course, there are thousands of situations in which one can become involved at any time. We have considered a wide variety of situations, and have come up with five of the more common situations. They include:

1. When you want something from someone
2. When someone wants something from you
3. Dealing with a difficult or aggressive person

4. A personal relationship situation

5. A situation dealing with a parent - child conflict

Although these examples are specific, keep in mind that the "Lewis Approach" will work in <u>any</u> situation involving relationships with a variety of people.

Each situation is covered separately and in two parts. Each part has two participants (people) who are discussing an issue. The first part is how most people converse today; the pain and trouble people experience <u>not</u> using our approach. In the second part, one of the participants is using the "Lewis Approach." You will clearly see how the conversation differs dramatically when even one of the participants uses the process. With the "Lewis Approach," you will also see a more open and clearer conversation between the people, who will feel much better about their conversation and each other.

As an added feature, the left side of the page illustrate the participants, in dialogue format. The right side of the page, which corresponds to the speaker, is explanatory narrative. This offers the best "live" view of the "Lewis Approach" in action. <u>You can use the same words and phrases right from these examples in a variety of your own situations</u>. Moreover, you will be able to <u>anticipate</u> the responses of the other person. This format offers the best and clearest picture of how our approach works. In short, you will get a "jump start" into the process and start to enjoy life more!

When You Want Something From Someone

Background: Shirley and Michelle, friends for a few years, relate well together. Shirley was invited to the wedding of Millie, a mutual friend of theirs. Shirley wants Michelle to attend the wedding with her. But Michelle has had recent arguments with Millie and does not want to attend her wedding.

First Scenario (Before - WITHOUT the approach)

Dialogue	Commentary
1. Shirley: We received an invitation to a wedding and the reception is at Millie's house. Do you want to ride with me?	1. Notice how Shirley phrased the question to where Michelle could answer either way, yes or no. This implies that Shirley is willing to accept either answer but she really is not. She wants Michelle to go.
2. Michelle: I'm not gonna go. Do you think I'm gonna go to her house? She thinks she's hot stuff.	2. Michelle indicated that she was not going, which produced feelings of guilt, and then began to justify why she wasn't going.
3. Shirley: Well, can't you go to the reception with me?	3. Again, Shirley is leaving it to where she can get a yes or

no answer but is not willing to accept a "no." At this point, she begins to pressure Michelle, who begins to feel some criticism.

4. Michelle: Why don't you just go and leave me out of it?

4. Michelle shows the effects of the criticism and begins to subtlety attack Shirley, via passive anger, as a defense to Shirley's pressuring. She is asking Shirley a question, begging an answer, rather than <u>telling</u> Shirley what she wants. (i.e. leave her out of it).

5. Shirley: Well, I don't want to go by myself. You're a good friend of mine. Can't you just go?

5. Notice here that, in response to Michelle's passive anger, Shirley appeals to Michelle's guilt by saying she is a good friend. Then she gives Michelle the same choice again, yes or no, but is only willing to accept the answer of "yes". Instead of telling Michelle what she wants her to do for her, Shirley continues to give Michelle choices that she really does not want Michelle

to have. This represents <u>dependency</u> on Shirley's part.

6. Michelle: Look, I told you I don't want to go so why don't you just leave me alone?

6. At this point, Michelle really begins to feel the pressure that she is being made to do something she does not want to do and takes a hard stand. Her emphatic resistance (passive anger) creates guilt in Michelle, which is reflected in her saying: "Why don't you just leave me alone." This statement also creates guilt for Shirley. It implies that Shirley is picking on Michelle or not treating her fairly.

7. Shirley: I do things for you, why don't you do things for me?

7. Shirley justifies her guilt and continues to give choices she does not want Michelle to have. She is also begging for a reason why Michelle should <u>not go</u>, instead of emphasizing why she should.

8. Michelle: Why don't you stop trying to control me. You are always trying to

8. Here, the issue is no longer Millie's wedding. The issue is "muddy" and their verbal

control people.

attacks and criticisms of each other begin to escalate. Again, it's <u>not</u> clear as to what each person really wants. Because of this, the communication is breaking down.

9. Shirley: You are the one who always wants to control. Remember that time you wanted to go to the beach and I wanted to go somewhere else and I went with you? You always want things your way. Why don't you think of other people sometime?

9. Again, they are even further away from the real issue: Millie's wedding. This is starting to get into a "good guy, bad guy" role where Shirley claims she treated Michelle well about the beach (i.e. good guy) but Michelle will not return the favor and go to the wedding (i.e. bad guy). They are also in a guilt- producing conversation.

10. Michelle: Your beginning to act just like Millie. That's why I don't like her.

10. This is definitely passive anger, which is squarely directed at Shirley. She is essentially saying that she is starting to not like Shirley with the same passion that she does not like Millie. Notice how Michelle puts the emphasis on Millie, not

Shirley, because Michelle does not want, or cannot, tell Shirley directly that she is irritating her. Michelle is essentially trying to <u>hide</u> her anger behind Millie's name.

11. Shirley: I don't blame Millie for not liking you.

11. Shirley is following Michelle's lead and is hiding her anger behind Millie's name. There is still no progress, not even close, on getting back to the issue of Shirley wanting Michelle to go to the wedding. They have probably forgotten the original conversation.

12. Michelle: You just do what you want to do. I don't care. I'm leaving!

12. The pressure of the conversation has driven Michelle to leave. She is emotionally exhausted and does not want to deal with it. Neither one feels too good right now. When they meet again, they will have some guilt feelings from this conversation. These guilt feelings are a result of the passive anger that each used.

As you can see, Shirley and Michelle are not happy with each other and are upset about what just transpired. A typical happening with people. No doubt you have had similar conversations. Many people end up feeling miserable after such conversations because they lack the skill or knowledge necessary to prevent it. Using our approach, we guarantee you will get more positive results. Here is the same situation, in dialog, using our approach.

First Scenario (After - WITH the approach)

Dialogue

Commentary

1. Shirley: We received an invitation to a wedding and the reception is at Millie's house. Ride with me.

1. Shirley is using steps 1, 2, & 4 of the process. She is telling Michelle what to do for her; telling Michelle to ride with her. She is also positioning herself well to deal with any resistance Michelle may have because she is only giving Michelle one choice: to ride with Shirley. Further, she is using the approach by accepting that Michelle has free will and may resist by saying no. She has the freedom to pursue what she wants without making Michelle feel criticized. Notice that Shirley

also just told Michelle the first time ("Three Times Rule") of what to do for her.

2. Michelle: I'm not going to go. Do you think I'm going to go to her house? She thinks she's hot stuff.

2. This is the same resistance as in the first example. Watch how Shirley handles it.

3. Shirley: I didn't know you felt that way. But I really want you to go with me to Millie's. So, come with me.

3. Shirley is using steps 3 & 4 of the process. Shirley shows understanding. Then, using direct anger, she instructs her to go to Millie's with her. She did not give Michelle a choice like "why don't you come" or "you should come". She just told her what to do for her. However, at the same time, she did not impose on Michelle free will to say yes or no. This is important. Notice that Shirley simply told Michelle the second time, of the "3 Times Rule," of what to do for her.

4. Michelle: Why don't you just leave me out of it. I don't want to go.

4. More resistance, but no criticism. Note that Michelle is in more of a problem

solving mode rather than in a defensive mode.

| 5. Shirley: I understand how you feel. But, it is important to me that you to go. So, go with me anyway. That would make me happy. | 5. Shirley is using steps 3, 4, & 5 of the process. Note that by her saying "go with me anyway," she is using the third time of the "3 Times Rule." Shirley is staying focused on the issue but not criticizing nor pressuring Michelle. She is providing emotional support for her and using a form of reward. Shirley still accepts Michelle's "free will." |

| 6. Michelle: Why should I make you happy? | 6. Michelle's question is to see what reason Shirley comes up with so she can "pick holes" in it. Michelle may also be trying to have Shirley persuaded her into going. |

| 7. Shirley: That's a good point. But tell me what is getting in your way of going with me. | 7. Shirley is using steps 3 & 5 of the process and did not answer the question. It appears that going to Millie's house is "8 feet" for Michelle. So Shirley is "lowering the |

bar" for Michelle. Michelle is also being helped to "get her problem out of her system."

8. Michelle: I already told you. Millie is not a good person and terrible to be around. She is stuck up and I don't want to be a part of that. I will just send the bride and groom a card.

8. Michelle is focusing on the issue, her not liking Millie, and proposes something else she would feel more comfortable doing. Compared to the previous example, we have a much more calm conversation on the same topic. By Shirley using the approach, the entire aura of the conversation has changed for the better.

9. Shirley: I appreciate that. Thanks for telling me that. But, it is really important to me that you go with me. So, work it out so that you can go. I would appreciate that.

9. Shirley is using steps 3, 6, & 7 of the process, focusing on what she wants. This disarms Michelle from the need to use passive anger or hostility and does not "fuel any fire." It also gives Michelle the feeling that she is being heard. Shirley is empowering Michelle to go with her by really *emphasizing the importance to her* that she go.

10. Michelle: Well, I don't even think you should go. She never treated you well either. She used to say things about you behind your back.

10. This is Michelle's last ditch effort: she is trying to manipulate Shirley and get her off track of what she wants.

11. Shirley: I knew you were going to say something like that. That really makes it hard for me when you say that. Change your mind. Don't even think of things like that. Just plan to go with me and I'd really feel good about that.

11. Shirley is using steps 8 & 9 of the process, using existing guilt to neutralize Michelle's resistance. Then, Shirley makes it unequivocally clear and gives directions to Michelle as to how to go along with her. She also again stressed the importance to her of Michelle going.

12. Michelle: Well, okay. I'll go. But if Millie starts acting up, I'm not going to go with you anywhere again.

12. Proper use of the approach has worked! Michelle made a conscious decision, out of her own "free will", to go and please Shirley. Michelle adds, "if something goes wrong she's not going anywhere with Shirley again," as a defense for her accepting to go.

13. Shirley: Thanks for

13. Shirley is using steps 10,

going along with me. I understand what you said about if things go wrong and stuff but let's just go and have a good time and not let things go wrong. I'd appreciate that.

3, & 1 of the process. Shirley immediately rewards Michelle for going with her. Shirley does not pay immediate attention to the other stuff Michelle said about Millie. Shirley understands and recognizes that she got what she wanted and that Michelle's comments are simply her defense in going along with her. She understands what Michelle said about the other stuff (use of step 3) and then told her what to do for her (i.e. "go and have a good time") (use of step 1).

See how much different this conversation is? Shirley used our approach and got Michelle to do something she originally did not want to do. Shirley never imposed herself on Michelle nor took away her "free will." Because of this, Michelle made a conscious decision to go along with Shirley and please her. Shirley simply used the approach fully and effectively.

In this example (and in those following) we have used virtually all of the 10 comprehensive steps of the process. You can use these examples directly, adjusting them to fit your particular situation. In a majority of situations, you will probably not need to go past steps 3 or 4 of the process. Most people will respond positively once you get to these steps.

What if the person does not seem to have the ability to do what you want them to do for you? Go back to step 5 of the process and repeat the remainder of the process. If the person still does not have the ability, then you would go to step 10A of the process. Realize that this person cannot do what you want at this time. So, try an alternate that they can do and which you are willing to accept.

Summary: Again, *the idea is to get what you want, without trying to force people to do things that they do not have the ability to do*. They may not have the ability to do what you want them to do on a particular day, but they may be able to do so at a later time, *if you don't alienate them*. The process does not alienate. Using our approach gives you the best possible chance of having the person please you freely.

When Someone Wants Something From You

Rita and Gary have dated a few times and seem to be moving toward a good relationship. However, Rita feels that Gary broke one too many promises and decides she no longer wants to see him. Gary wants to continue the relationship and is pursuing Rita vigorously: He calls her almost daily, even calling her parents and friends trying to reach her. Rita wants him to stop bugging her.

Second Scenario (Before - WITHOUT the approach)

Dialogue

Commentary

1. Gary: Rita. I'm glad you answered the phone. This is Gary. I have been trying to get a hold of you for a long time now. How come you have not been returning my calls?

1. Gary begins as if everything is okay. He starts with a question which makes Rita defensive. He is choosing to ignore that there is a problem.

2. Rita: I told you that I did not want to talk to you anymore! Why are you calling me?

2. Rita shows she is irritated with Gary, but is taking a dependent position: she expects him to know what she wants without telling him. She raises a question which opens the issue up for a debate that Rita does not want. She is using passive

anger, expecting him to "figure out" what to do without telling him.

3. Gary: Why are you so mean to me? Don't you know I care about you?

3. Gary, like Rita, raises issues that he does not want the answer to. He is in a dependent role, counting on capitalizing on her feelings of guilt; a "guilt trip," asking: "Why are you so mean to me?"

4. Rita: If you cared about me, why would you keep bothering me? And don't you dare keep calling my parents and friends asking where I am! Who do you think you are?

4. Rita is using "two anger's at once" ("don't you dare!..."). She tells him not to dare, one anger, said with emotion, the second anger. Then she uses more passive anger, asking him more questions to which she does not want the answer (i.e. "who do you think you are?"). This passive anger perpetuates a conversation she does <u>not</u> want to have.

5. Gary: I only called them because you wouldn't answer my call. You should have called me back. All I want to do is talk to you.

5. Gary responds to her question. This only irritates Rita more because she does really not want an answer to the question. She just wants

What is the matter with that?

him to stop calling. Gary is responding as if Rita is the cause of the problem. He then tries to justify his calls and thinks that Rita should accept that. Basically he is implying that _he_ is the authority on what she should and should not do.

6. Rita: Look, I told you I don't want to have anything to do with you. We are finished and I don't ever want to talk to you again. Can't you get that into your thick head? Why can't you just be a man and deal with it?

6. This _sounds_ like Rita is being decisive and knows what she wants. But she is not. She is still dependent: counting on him to understand what she is saying, accept it, and go along with it. She is also trying to take away Gary's "free will" by forcing him to go along with her. Then she complicates the situation by criticizing him: "...get it into your thick head ... and deal with it?" This verbal attack would "fuel his fire" causing him to resist more, purposely upset Rita, or criticize her back. Either of these would make the situation worse for Rita.

7. Gary: You don't mean what you are saying. You are just feeling hurt. All I need to do is just talk to you and you will be all right. Okay?

7. Gary knows that Rita feels angry, but he is not facing what she is telling him. He thinks he can straighten her out by just talking to her. But that will only upset Rita more.

8. Rita: Why do you keep calling me? Can't you just stop calling and leave me alone?

8. Again, Rita asks questions she does not really want answered. She is still not focusing on what she really wants. She believes that she is being decisive in telling him not to call, yet she is asking for reasons why he still calls. This gives Gary a false feeling of hope that if he comes up with the right reasons, then it's okay to call.

9. Gary: I'm calling you because I know you have trouble getting close. You just have some problems relating to men. So, why don't we just go out to dinner so we can talk things out? You just need to get out. That's what wrong with you.

9. Gary never takes responsibility for himself; he may even be in denial. He is also attacking Rita by using passive anger and being judgmental. It sounds as though he cares, but his accusations are pressuring her, that something is wrong

with her.

10. Rita: I'm not gonna talk to you any more and you better not call me again. Bye! (She slams the phone down).	10. Rita believes that she actually told him what to do. She <u>hopes</u> that he won't call, yet fears he will. Essentially, she is still dependent upon Gary not to call, feeling that she does not have the power to influence him not calling. She will, therefore, feel anxiety about this for a while.

This is a typical example of how people relate to each other. Each person is dependent on the other to respond the way <u>they</u> want them to respond, but without telling them how to do so. Gary will <u>not</u> respond the way Rita wants him to, which causes anger in Rita. Why doesn't Gary meet Rita's needs? Firstly, Gary does not <u>know</u> what to do to meet her needs. He only knows she is angry with him. Rita, being dependent, never tells him what to do for her. Secondly, and most importantly, Gary is focused on his own needs. Neither Rita nor Gary tells the other <u>exactly what to do</u> to meet their respective needs. Neither one will get what they want.

Let's now see how you how Rita uses the approach in this book to get what she wants in this same situation. Her objective is to have him please her by doing things <u>her</u> way and helping her to get on with her life without him.

Second Scenario (After - WITH the approach)

Dialogue

Commentary

1. Gary: Rita. I'm glad you answered the phone. This is Gary. I have been trying to get a hold of you for a long time now. How come you have not been returning my calls?

1. Same as in example above.

2. Rita: Thanks for calling. When we last talked, I told you that I wanted us not to see each other anymore. I still would like that. So let's work it out that we not see each other any more.

2. Rita is using steps 1, 2, & 4 of the process. She is telling Gary what she wants and how to please her. She is also telling him the first of the "3 Times Rule."

3. Gary: Why are you saying that? Don't you know that I really like you? Why are you being mean?

3. Gary is in a dependent position, asking questions and implying that Rita is wrong. ("don't you know I care about you?") He is trying to make Rita feel guilty. He also is implying that since he cares about her, she must care about him. This imposes on Rita's "free will." Essentially, he is trying to manipulate her.

215

4. Rita: I understand how you feel and I appreciate you telling me that. But, go along with me and let's not see each other.

4. Rita is using steps 3 & 4 of the process. She tells him that she <u>understands</u> how he feels. This will help him to listen to what she says. It will also reduce his aggressive drive to have her understand what he says. Then, she uses the second of the "3 Times Rule."

5. Gary: Why don't you just go out with me? We'll go out and have a nice dinner, talk things over, and you will see how much I care. Everything will work out. Okay?

5. Gary did not respond to anything Rita said. Gary may sound confident, but he is anticipating Rita's resistance.

6. Rita: That's really nice of you to suggest that we do that. But, this is really important to me that I have it my way. So, let's not go out together anymore. I'd appreciate that.

6. Rita is using steps 3 & 4 again of the process. Instead of rejecting him, she tells him that she understands what he is saying. This "disarms" Gary's drive to try to get Rita to go out with him. At the same time, it shows her understanding of what he is saying, reducing Gary's resistance. Rita stresses the <u>importance</u> the issue has to

her. This taps into and strengthens Gary's "desire to please." Then, she uses the third of the "3 Times Rule," again telling him what to do for her. Her use of direct anger will start to outweigh his use of passive anger. This automatically helps Gary work through the problem.

7. Gary: Why are you doing this to me? All I want to do is get back together with you and work things out. Is there anything wrong with that? Why don't you just give me one more chance?

7. Gary is trying to manipulate Rita and impose "guilt trip" on her. He tries to sound like he is the "good guy" being victimized by Rita. Unknowingly, he is still in a dependent position by asking her two more questions.

8.Rita:You are raising some good questions and I understand what you are saying. But, what you want me to do is more than I can do. So, go along with me on this and let's not see each other. That would make me feel

8. Rita is using a combination of steps 3, 5, & 7 of the process. She rewards Gary for sharing what he is thinking and lets him know that he is understood. This will significantly reduce Gary's

good.

drive to pressure her. Rita then uses step 5 telling Gary that what he wants her to do is more than she can do (i.e. "8 Feet"). Lastly, she uses step 7 of the process by telling him what to do for her. She continues to tell Gary, very clearly, what to do for her and how to please her.

9. Gary: You know, you are a wench! I should have listened to my friends when they said that you were no good. Wait until I see your friends at work. I am going to tell them what you are doing to me and what kind of person you are.

9. Gary begins to face reality. It may sound like he is getting tough with her, but he is really coming to the end of his effort and is about to change his position. But he also criticizes her in an attempt to shake her from her position. If he is successful, and she gets angry in a passive way (i.e. criticizes him back), then it opens the door for Gary to be more hostile and feel justified doing so. This will also create unnecessary guilt for Rita which Gary will automatically use against

her to strengthen his position. (People do this often when their progress is being stopped, and they don't even know it).

10. Rita: I never thought you would say that. That really hurts my feelings. Don't say things like that to me. Be nice to me and go along with me. Let me have it all my way so that we don't see each other. Do that for me.

10. Rita is using steps 8 & 9 of the process. She first uses step 8 of the process. This guilt will greatly reduce his drive for additional verbal attacks. Then, Rita uses step 9 of the process. She knows that direct anger is stronger than passive anger so she becomes more positive selfish, uses more direct anger, and really begins to tell Gary to do everything for her.

11. Gary: I don't think I can stop seeing you. I really care for you that much. Let me think about it.

11. Gary has made a concession and has stopped criticizing her, focusing on what he can, or, in this case, cannot do. He has shifted from using "you" words to "I" words. His response was set up by Rita instructing Gary on what she wanted, not rejecting

him. She also focused on understanding what he said and then telling him how to please her. She never criticized or challenged him.

12. Rita: Gary, thanks for doing that for me. That really makes me happy. I really appreciate that.

12. Rita is using step 10 of the process. She is rewarding him, which relieves any guilt she may have as a result of her using direct anger. This also keeps her from getting back into the discussion again. Additionally, she is acknowledging that she has gotten what she wanted. This helps Gary to completely work through this change and give her what she wants. Gary may be ambivalent about this but by Rita using this step, she is helping him through his ambivalence.

13. Gary: Why don't you make me feel good and see me again and let me have what I want?

13. This is Gary's absolute "last gasp" to try to get back into the process, even though he had changed his

position and decided to go along with her. He is also making sure, in his mind, that Rita really wants this. He is looking to see if there is any weakness is what she wants.

14. Rita: Gary, don't ask me to do that. Go out of your way for me and let me have this all my way. Make me happy. Do that for me and let's keep this the way we decided. I'd appreciate that.

14. Rita stays with using the approach and not getting back into the issue. She is able to use step 9 of the process again by using direct anger: wanting everything her way; not being rejecting; and not taking away his "free will." Unequivocally, it directs him to do for her what she wants him to do.

15. Gary: Okay. I can see this really means a lot to you. I'll be seeing you around.

15. He has decided to accept what Rita wants him to do without a lot of angry feelings towards her.

16. Rita: Thanks Gary. That makes me feel good.

16. Rita again uses step 10 of the process. She rewards him for pleasing her.

See how much different this conversation went when Rita used our approach! Notice how she never tried to criticize, reason, explain, coerce, convince, or do anything else with Gary. She remained focused on what she wanted and instructed Gary on how to please her. From the very first steps, she decided what she wanted and <u>stuck with that decision throughout the process</u>. Now both Rita and Gary feel much better about each other.

A key point to remember: Rita never rejected Gary. If she had, this would have motivated him to fight harder to try to get her to change her mind.

Typically, when someone is angry with another person, they will reject him or her. The one being rejected then has a tendency to think: "If I can stop him/her from being angry with me, he/she will accept me." To do this, they try to lay "guilt trips" on the other person or manipulate, verbally attack, or force the person to stop being angry with them. This never works. It only creates arguments and bad feelings in both parties. If you find yourself in a situation similar to the above example, use the "Lewis Approach" fully and enjoy the same type of smooth results which Rita achieved.

Dealing With A Difficult Or Aggressive Person

Using the "Lewis Approach" will also help you to deal with people who are aggressive or especially difficult.

There are a few very important things to keep in mind when dealing with such individuals. These people tend to be very insecure inside. They may appear tough on the surface, but we are certain that every one of them has had problems with how they interact with and relate to others. They often feel inadequate and insecure, which causes them to act aggressively to hide their problems or not have to deal with other people. Once you transcend their aggression, you see their warmth and caring underneath that mask of protection. This is revealed in the Christmas story about Scrooge. They seem tough and callous, but when they no longer need their defenses, their tenderness and thoughtfulness are revealed. This mask of aggressiveness can be a part of many people - including family and friends.

Sometimes very nice and soft-spoken people may become "monsters" in certain situations when they lose control. Their voice gets louder, their speech gets faster, their movements get quicker, and their body language becomes more animated or physical. These are signs of losing control and becoming difficult or aggressive. At one point or another, all of us may become a difficult or aggressive person, if our feelings have been hurt deeply enough or our progress blocked too often. When this happens, we are more susceptible to lashing out at others.

There are specific principles to keep in mind when dealing with aggressive or difficult people. Obviously, such individuals are not getting what they need or want. Maybe someone rejected or disappointed them and they now lash out at you. A variety of situations can cause this. The bottom line is these people are emotionally out of control. Often they become irrational and resist any attempts to reason. This may frustrate you; in turn, you can also become unreasonable as well because your progress is blocked. Inevitably, an argument could ensue. But, as we have stated in this book, our approach does not involve reasoning, so this would not be a problem if you use our approach.

To summarize, think of the following specific and important points as a "lifeline" to success when dealing with people who act aggressively or irrational. This will keep you from getting upset and allow you to help the other person to gain control of his or her emotions.

Specific points:

1. Use one anger at a time
2. See yourself as perfect (not necessarily correct)
3. As soon as you sense someone being aggressive, do <u>not</u> ask or answer any questions. Use only statements and instructions (direct anger) and be understanding.

4. The difficult or aggressive person must give you the power to help them. Accept this power to take responsibility of leading the conversation in a positive direction. Your goal is to help the person solve his or her problem or regain control of his or her emotions, not to get your needs met. Position yourself to be in control of the interaction with others by focusing on what they are saying. Do this by wanting everything your way and using "HTE". Have Them Explain (what they are saying or what they mean). The person must have the ability to do what you want (i.e., jump "8 Feet").

5. Don't give choices (do allow them their "free will"). Simply tell them what to do for you and how to please you.

6. When they do what you want them to do, reward them as often as possible. This reduces their insecurity as well as their need to verbally attack you.

These key points are similar to the ten comprehensive steps of our approach. But we wanted to highlight them again to stress their particular importance.

The following example relates to dealing with difficult people: Don and Keith are friendly neighbor's in an apartment complex. Don and his children live in the unit above Keith's. Don, an easygoing guy, is known as a reasonable and approachable person. Keith is nice and cordial as well, but he has been known to have a somewhat wild streak in him and can sometimes be very opinionated. He speaks his mind and can be unreasonable at times. Overall, they have gotten along pretty well in the past.

Don's kids sometimes play in the house, particularly on rainy or cold days. This creates normal noises that children make: such as running, jumping, bumping, etc. Keith is facing financial difficulties and his "fuse" is a little shorter than usual. These noises irritate him and he decides to visit Don's unit.

Third Scenario (Before - WITHOUT the approach)

Dialogue

Commentary

1. Keith: (Keith goes to Don's unit and bangs on the door. When Don opens it, Keith says:) <u>Don, would you shut those darn kids up?!</u> They have been making noises for hours! How do you expect anyone to get any rest with all that racket going on!

1. Keith goes to Don in a state of passive anger. He bangs on his door and confronts him, which will cause Don to be defensive. But Keith is unclear as to what he wants when he asks: "Who can get rest with all that racket going on?" This is typical of how the difficult or aggressive person behaves.

2. Don: What do you mean? My kids haven't been making any more

2. Don immediately becomes defensive. Even if Don thought his kids were making

noise than any other children.

excessive noise, he would play it down for fear of more of an attack if he admitted this. Keith, using passive anger, got him the opposite results of what he wanted.

3. Keith: Oh yes they have! They are always making noise! They have been making noise for months. I have just gotten fed up with it.

3. Keith now takes Don's resistance as a challenge, which increases Keith's passive anger and causes him to be more aggressive and confrontational. To strengthen his argument, Keith exaggerates the situation by saying that this noise has been going on for months. This is to hurt Don's feelings. The verbal attack is personal at this point.

4. Don: Yeah, well if you feel that way, I am going to complain every time you play your music loud. And when your kids are outside, they disturb people with their yelling and screaming too. You're not such a saint yourself.

4. Don switches position from defensive to attacking, (i.e. he will complain when Keith plays his music); and then he verbally attacks Keith's kids. Using sarcasm, he tells Keith he "is no saint." This is a passive way of telling Keith he is a problem. This conversation is clearly getting

worse.

5. Keith: I knew when I first met you that you were going to be a problem. Nobody around here likes you because you are such a problem. You never think about anybody else. You only think of yourself.

5. Keith now resorts to personal (verbal) attacks on Don and is completely off the topic. Keith's comments are designed to hurt and attack. He also tries to further justify his position by saying others feel as he does. Keith is thus trying to manipulate Don by "teaming up" with other people who are not present.

6. Don: I have friends around here. I talk to Clifford a lot.

6. Don tries to defend himself again. More noteworthy, he is trying to prove Keith wrong.

7. Keith: Who, that drunk? All you can do is run around with losers! And he can't take care of his kids either. They are going to be school drop outs before long.

7. Now Keith attacks Clifford as well and he insults Don again (saying he hangs around with losers). This is to hurt Don's feelings. He may not even mean what he says, but he's trying to erase the fact that Don has friends and attacks Clifford's character. But Keith is "off track" and has lost focus. Still no progress about the kids.

8. Don: Why don't you just shut up and leave and go on back to your own place?

8. Don tries to end this conversation by sounding tough. The conversation has gone beyond what Don wants to handle at this point. This is also a rejection of Keith, which makes Keith more hostile. Don, in essence, is blocking Keith's progress: Keith is not getting what he wants.

9. Keith: Oh, you're gonna make me? Why don't you come out here and make me?

9. At this point, Keith recognizes his words are not working. He feels like a failure, which increases his feelings of insecurity and inadequacy. As a result, he turns to physical threats to reduce these negative feelings. But Keith is in a dependent position and is acting impulsively. His physical threat represents passive anger, although it may sound like strong anger, because that anger is not designed to get anything for himself. It is only designed to hurt. But, that was not what he wanted in the first place. He wanted

to have Don's kids stop making noise, remember?

10. Don: If you don't get out of here and quit harassing me, I am going to call the police. You just get out of my face.	10. Don is trying to end the pressure this conversation is causing him. So he threatens Keith with the police. Don is also dealing from a weak position here, giving the controls over to Keith. If Keith doesn't do something, he will take action and call the police. This puts Keith in control of Don's next actions.
11. Keith: Oh yeah, that's how you want to play it, huh. Two can play the same game, you jerk.	11. Keith now makes an idle threat to "save face." Neither wants to be physical or deal with the police. Further, neither Don nor Keith is taking responsibility for their role in this conversation. Each blames the other for being the "bad person." This makes it impossible for either one to get their needs met. Each must take the responsibility of getting their own needs met.
12. Don: (Don slams the door angrily).	12. Don takes out his aggression on the door

because there are fewer consequences. Additionally, it provides him a transition from an intense emotion to a less intense emotion. But Don's anger and frustration are still there and will create feelings of anxiety or depression that could linger.

13. Keith: You jerk! (Keith bangs on Don's door before he walks away).

13. Keith also takes his aggression out on the door, which provides him too with a transition. But he will also have feelings of anger, anxiety, or depression that will linger. For both Keith and Don, the "door banging" was their way of acknowledging the end of the confrontation.

This is typical of passive anger conversations in confrontational situations. These two people are very angry with each other and almost came to blows. The next time they see each other, they will be uncomfortable and uneasy, wondering how the other will react. Each may believe they were right and justified in what they said or did. But the use of passive anger is painful to both parties, who will later end up feeling guilty for their behavior.

Anytime people use passive anger, they will feel guilty. This explains why, after people quarrel, there is a natural desire for reconciliation. Consciously or subconsciously, people want to be free of their guilt feelings.

Further, there is a natural tendency to feel anxious or depressed after one expresses intense amounts of passive anger. People will secretly blame themselves, wondering what they could have done differently. Then both tend to withdraw and resist further interaction with the other person.

The most important issue here is: Did either of them get what they wanted? Did Keith get Don to have his kids stop making noise? Is Don happy with Keith? Is Keith happy with Don? Both may have lost a friend that the other may need to count on in the future.

Lastly, how do you think Don's kids feel? With all of that aggressive talk and yelling between Keith and their father, you can be sure they too feel anxious and nervous about what happened. They may also wonder whether they may be able to play with Keith's kids or not, as they were also friends.

Now let's see how Don uses the "Lewis Approach", in the same scenario, to get totally different (positive) results with Keith.

Third Scenario (After - WITH the approach)

Dialogue	Commentary
1. Keith: (Keith goes to Don's unit and bangs on the door. When Don opens it, Keith says:) <u>Don, would you shut those darn kids up?!</u> They have been making noises for hours! How do you expect anyone to get any rest with all that racket going on!	1. This is the same thing Keith said in the "before" example. See above.
2. Don: Tell me what you mean.	2. Don is using steps 1 & 2 of the process. He is using step 1 by utilizing "HTE": "Have Them Explain." Keith insulted Don by the way he talked to him. Don uses "HTE" to take control of the conversation. Keith will now be "answering" to Don, whether he realizes it or not. Using direct anger, Don will get clarification from Keith about what he specifically wants. Because of how Keith started the situation, Don will anticipate resistance on

3. Keith: You know what I mean. Your kids are always making noise. They have been making noise for months and I have gotten fed up with it. Why don't you shut those kids up?

3. Keith followed Don's direct anger instruction. But, Keith is still confronting to solicit opposition from Don, in order to justify his continuing to verbally strikeout. Keith needs to feel Don is deserving of his verbal attacks and passive anger.

4. Don: I can see that this is really bothering you and can understand how you feel. But, talk nicer to me and tell me more about what is troubling you.

4. Don is using steps 3 & 4 of the process. Don uses step 3 (telling Keith he understands how he feels.) This reduces Keith's drive to continue his verbal attack. Don uses step 4 (the first of the "3 Times Rule"), telling Keith to be nicer to him and to tell him more about what is bothering him. This gives Keith directions as how to please Don plus the feeling that Don cares about him. Additionally, this step helps provide Keith the structure he needs to get control of his emotions. Don's use of direct anger also

provides Keith with security, which will reduce his need to express impulsive behavior.

5. Keith: Well, I have been having some financial problems and other troubles and I have to come home and hear all that noise that your kids make when they play in the house. I'm not going to put up with that. You are going to have to do something with those kids.

5. Keith begins to talk about the <u>real</u> issues bothering him: his financial problems and others. He explains why he cannot tolerate the playing noise. But, you can see a change in Keith, a result of Don using the approach in this book. Keith went from being aggressive and confrontational to being open to discuss rationally what is bothering him. But he is still upset, as he tells Don he has to do something about his kids making noise.

6. Don: I understand how you feel and I can appreciate you telling me that. But, tell me why this is bothering you today.

6. Don is using steps 3 & 4 of the process again. First, Don uses step 3 by understanding what Keith is saying. This conveys to Keith he is being heard, which will diminish his desire to verbally attack or resist Don. Then Don uses step 4 (the second of the "3 Times Rule"), telling Keith to

tell him why this is bothering him today. This provides clarification for both Don and Keith as it helps them to see what the real problem is. Step 4 continues to clarify the problem (i.e. Keith's financial difficulties and other troubles.)

7. Keith: Well, I just can't put up with it today. I just don't feel good. Those kids are just bothering me. I know kids make noise but I am just not able to deal with it today.

7. It is clear what is really bothering Keith. He is not feeling well and acknowledges that he understands kids make noise. Because of how he feels, he simply can't take the noise today.

8. Don: Well, tell me what you would like for me to do that would work out for me.

8. Don is using steps 5 & 7 of the process. Don uses step 7, which tells Keith what he wants him to do. Essentially, Don is instructing Keith as to what he wants him to do but which would also work out for Don. Don is in control of his life space, protective of his children, and addresses Keith's problem. The decision will be up to Don: he will either go along with what Keith tells

him or instruct him to make another option. This represents the "8 Feet" part of this process. Don will be in control of determining whether Keith's response represents "8 feet" for him or not. This is how step 5 is utilized in this situation.

9. Keith: Well, maybe you could not have them play so much in the house or maybe they could play at different times.

9. At this point, Keith has just followed Don's instruction and is attempting to find an acceptable solution to the problem; one that would work for both. Notice how the dynamics of the conversation have completely changed: a result of <u>Don</u> using our approach. Keith now takes an active role in solving his own problem instead of being angry (in a passive way) or being confrontational.

10. Don: I'll let them play until 9:00 p.m. and then I'll have them stop. Let's work it out that way.

10. Don is using step 7 of the process. He is keeping control of getting his own needs met and expressing them clearly. He uses direct anger: "Let's work it out that way". This

instructional statement makes it clear what Don wants Keith to do. This also empowers Keith to please Don because he knows clearly what will work for Don, (the 9:00 p.m. time); at the same time Keith's issue is addressed.

11. Keith: 9:00 p.m.???
Can't you get them to stop sooner than that? They'd make too much noise at that late time.

11. Keith is in a dependent position, responding to what Don said, not what he (Keith) wants. He does this by raising a question, which is passive anger. The phrase, "Can't you get them to stop sooner?", is dependent because this question gives Don a choice, which he does not want Don to have. (Note: If Don does not correctly handle what Keith asked him, it could lead to an argument.)

12. Don: *Keith, I knew you were going to say that.* (Said with emphasis). Let the kids play until 9:00 p.m. and then stop. Do that for me.

12. Don is using steps 8 & 9 of the process. Don uses step 8: *"Keith, I knew you were going to say that."* This is designed to generate Keith's natural feelings of guilt as a result of him using passive anger

towards Don. It will also reduce Keith's drive to express passive anger and resist. Then Don uses step 9: "Let the kids play until 9:00 p.m." and "Do that for me". These two direct anger statements give clear instructions as to what Don wants Keith to do for him. It provides clarity to Keith, tapping into Keith's innate desire to please. Keith may do it for Don but he won't do it just to do it. This makes it easier for Keith to go along with Don and please him.

13. Keith: Okay, that will be fine. 9:00 p.m.
but not a minute later.

13. Don helped Keith to have the strength to do this and please him. By Don being clear on what he wanted and using direct anger to instruct Keith how to please him, it helped Keith to decide what he wanted and was able to do. Additionally, Keith made this decision because he wanted to make it, not because he was forced to. His comment about, "...but not a minute later." was his way of

acknowledging the conclusion of the problem and its solution. Despite his comment, he is still going along with Don.

14. Don: Thanks Keith. I'm glad we worked this out. I'll talk to you later.

14. Don is using step 10 of the process. He acknowledges the situation worked out and that he got what he wanted. He rewards Keith by thanking him for doing this. This does two things. It acknowledges that Don got what he wanted and that he is pleased. Secondly, it relieves Don of any remnants of guilt he may have from using direct anger. Notice that Don did not respond to Keith's comment about, "...not a minute later." because he had already got what he wanted. Don recognized this as Keith's way of acknowledging that his problem is solved.

15. Keith: All right. See you later.

15. This statement allows Keith to get rid of the guilt he would have as a result of his using passive anger. It helps

him to verbally acknowledge
that a resolution has been
reached.

Notice how much different this conversation is from the earlier example which was hostile and confrontational. With Don using our approach in this book, the conversation changed completely, and for the better. Keith never got angry or upset and was able to stay calm as Don went through the process. Don used the steps of the process very well. He knew from the beginning that Keith had a problem by the way he banged on his door and aggressively and rudely told Don to "shut his kids up." Don knew not to take on the other person's problem. Instead, he immediately and naturally started to use the steps of the process which worked very well!

Don used direct anger particularly well and effectively. He gave Keith clear and concise instructions on how to please him, which helped Keith gather the strength to calm himself and become more reasonable. Keith went from being aggressive and confrontational to freely offering solutions to solve the problem.

Further, both Don and Keith felt much better after this conversation and continued on with their evening plans normally, without having ill feelings about the other. When they meet later, they will be in a very good position to speak easily and comfortably with each other.

Finally, neither Don's nor Keith's kids will be negatively effected by this conversation. Their kids will be able to play with each other, free of worry or concern about their parents' relationship. Their relationship as friends and playmates remains unaffected.

Clearly, we can see how the "Lewis Approach" worked in solving a problem between two people, in this case, friendly neighbors. We are confident that you will be able to use our approach just as effectively and keep your life as smooth and as enjoyable as possible.

Dealing With a Personal Relationship

This is the most popular example. Everyone is concerned with the dynamics of relationships and how they work. We know from our experience that the "Lewis Approach" works best in intimate relationships. Of course, the best situation is to become involved in a relationship where both share similar values. This sets a more positive foundation for success.

Don't try to change the other person - your spouse, mate, significant other, or anyone. Only tell them _how_ to meet your needs. Our approach will work even with those who do not share the same value system. _Regardless of whether two peoples value systems are similar or not, our approach will be effective in solving problems and helping people to grow together._

Example: Background information. Sylvia and Jeff are a married couple who enjoy a good relationship overall, but have some problems in relating. Right now Sylvia thinks Jeff spends too much time with his friend Eddie watching sports, playing cards, and "hanging out." Sylvia does not feel comfortable with Jeff spending so much time with Eddie; she wants Jeff to spend more time at home with her. On the other hand, Jeff thinks that Sylvia spends too much time with _her_ family, and that she cares more for them than she does for him. He claims that every time Sylvia's family has a problem, she leaves him and rushes there to help them. In this scenario, Jeff has just arrived home, late, and Sylvia plans to confront him.

Fourth Scenario (Before - WITHOUT the approach)

Dialogue	Commentary
1. Sylvia: Finally, you're home. Where were you, at Eddie's again?	1. Sylvia is confrontational by the way she phrases her question. It's as if she is preparing herself to really give Jeff a hard time about coming home late.
2. Jeff: Why do you keep getting on my case about Eddie? You just don't want me to have a nice time with my friend. You don't like any of my friends, do you?	2. Jeff begins his response by being defensive and then becomes accusatory. A typical response.
3. Sylvia: All you think about is your friends. You never think about me. Why don't you ever think about coming straight home and fixing things around the house?	3. At this point, it is difficult to figure out what Sylvia is really upset about. Is it Eddie? About fixing things around the house? About coming home at a certain time? This uncertainty by Sylvia, and her lack of clearly stating what she wants from Jeff, represents dependency, which causes the conversation to worsen.

4. Jeff: Me not think about you? You don't think about me. Why is it that every time your family has a problem, you go over there to help them and totally forget about me? Then you have the nerve to complain about me visiting my friend.

4. Jeff is on the defensive and then accusatory. He asserts that Sylvia is hypocritical: she is not thinking of him and that she is putting her family ahead of him. Here are two people choosing to be dependent on each other; although neither is actually aware of this. Neither takes responsibility to tell the other how to please. Rather, they just attack each other (in the form of angry questions)for not meeting the others' needs. It is as if each is intentionally trying to hurt the other.

5. Sylvia: You know what your problem is? You don't like my family because we are so close. You think you know how to get close? Why do you think your family doesn't come over to see you or how come you don't ever go over to see them? Your family can't stand you. What do you think the reason was for you leaving

5. Sylvia feels hurt because Jeff is attacking an area that Sylvia holds dear, her family. As a result, Sylvia's anger begins to intensify. She becomes more aggressive and escalates her accusations and verbal attacks. Is this what Sylvia was originally upset about? No! These two are entering

your family when you turned 18 years old?

6. Jeff: You never were able to understand my family. Remember when we were going to visit my mother and you said you did not want to go over there because my brother was a drunk? And you never did like my family's friends either. Why didn't you ever want to visit with my family? Do you think you are too good for my family, Miss Prissy?

7. Sylvia: Who can understand crazy people like your family anyway? And don't call me prissy you over weight pig. You and Eddie just bum around and are up to no good. You two will never amount to anything. I thought I was married to a responsible man. Come to find out I am married to a no good bum.

areas in which they do not need to be.

6. Jeff's defensiveness is shown by his verbal attacks on Sylvia. (A common type of defense: verbally attack the other person.) Jeff attacks Sylvia by questioning her intents about his family and makes it sound as if she is the person with a problem. Then, he becomes condescending by calling her "Miss Prissy."

7. Clearly the conversation is deteriorating. It is still very unclear as to what is really bothering Sylvia. By harshly criticizing Jeff, it appears her sole intent is to cut him down and hurt his feelings. She does this in response to Jeff's comment about "Miss Prissy." Neither is feeling too good about the other. In fact, they appear extremely angry with each other.

8. Jeff: Well, if you don't like me why don't you just pack up your bags and leave. I work hard all day. I don't have to come home and listen to this stuff. I don't need it.

8. Here's the ultimatum that always seems to happen in many relationships. Jeff, upset with Sylvia, challenges her to leave. In essence, he rejects her. A very painful form of passive anger: Rejection, a very strong attempt to control the other person, to force them into submission. But submission into what? What is Jeff communicating to Sylvia that he wants her to do? By Jeff's threatening, he is trying to force her to stop doing what she is doing without telling her <u>exactly</u> what that is. He is trying to put fear into her. He can now no longer tolerate this discussion. (Incidentally, many divorces begin with similar conversations).

9. Sylvia: Don't you threaten me. Who do you think you are? You think you can come in here after I have made your dinner and cleaned the

9. Sylvia responds to Jeff's threat with a threat of her own. First, she tries to justify hurting Jeff by stating that she does everything

house and you just stay out late with your loser friend, come home with beer on your breath and disrespect me like that? Do you want me to get an attorney on you?

10. Jeff: If you want an attorney you go right ahead and get one. I don't care.

around the house and he hurts her with threats and mistreatment. Then she threatens him with an attorney. Each person is trying to stop the pain they are experiencing here. They are trying to force each other to stop.

10. Jeff "calls her bluff" and tells her to call an attorney. He is trying to get her to stop the pressure that she is putting on him in this conversation. Even though it sounds as though he is in charge, he is still very much in a dependent role. He is not giving her a clear message of what to do for him; thereby maintaining his dependent role. What he is trying to settle is not whether they should be together or not, but some other unidentified issue yet to be discussed in this conversation. Jeff doesn't know what he wants, although he may sound as if

he does. We know Sylvia doesn't want an attorney either. They both just want to solve "the problem" but don't know how.

11. Sylvia: I'm not gonna talk to you any more. Forget you. (Sylvia walks out and slams the door.)

11. Sylvia can't handle the pressure and stress of the confrontation. To avoid the pressure, she leaves. Not only did she not get her original issue cleared up, but now has this situation to add to her list. This is more work for her to deal with and, at least temporarily, will decrease the quality of her life. She will not feel good about what just happened.

12. Jeff: (Yelling) You're always nagging! That's what I don't like about you!

12 Jeff says this because he is feeling guilty for hurting Sylvia and causing her to leave the room. Even though his intellect may tell him his remarks were justified, his subconscious mind automatically reminds him of the passive anger he used in the conversation,

which causes his guilt. (This is an automatic process with people and many don't even realize this is happening.) He exclaims something is wrong about Sylvia (i.e. you're always nagging, etc.) in an attempt to get rid of this guilt. Like Sylvia, Jeff has another problem to deal with that will effect the quality of his life, at least in the short term.

This example is typical of how most people relate. Notice how each is dependent on the other to respond the way she or he wants them to, <u>without telling the other how to do this</u>. This dependency is a major cause of these kinds of conversations. Often, people do not even realize they are dependent at all. People want others to understand what bothered them without verbalizing their feelings. This is a weak position. While their issues did present themselves briefly in this conversation, neither of them communicated to the other what they wanted the other person to <u>do</u> for them, or <u>how</u> to deal with the issues.

Taking this one step further, the reality is that the "real issues" were not discussed. If they had focused on one topic, they would have automatically honed in on the one effecting their lives now - and would be closer to resolving that.

Using the "Lewis Approach" <u>automatically</u> brings these issues to the forefront, without imposing on the other person. It offers the best possible chance to work out issues and be happier as a result.

Let's see the same conversation using the "Lewis Approach" and getting totally different (positive) results. Remember, Jeff is coming home to a "whirlwind" anger (passive anger) and he doesn't want to have to fight off the verbal attacks. His objective is to avoid passive hostility which will adversely effect the quality of his life but, simultaneously, allow Sylvia her free will and expression.

Fourth Scenario (After - WITH the approach)

Dialogue	Commentary
1. Sylvia: Finally, you're home. Where were you, at Eddie's again?	1. This is the same thing Sylvia said in the "before" example.
2. Jeff: I'm not sure why you are asking me that. Tell me why you are asking me.	2. Jeff is using steps 1 & 2 of the process. He senses Sylvia's anger, but decides he does not want to get into a hassle with her. This represents what he wants: no hassle. Because Sylvia is verbally attacking him, Jeff

uses "HTE": "Have Them Explain." In the process, he takes charge of the situation to help Sylvia stabilize herself. This represents step 1 of the process. Jeff will anticipate resistance on Sylvia's part. (Jeff using step 2.) Notice how Jeff is not taking on Sylvia's problem. To do this, Jeff must see himself as "perfect the way he is" and want things his way. He is accepting that Sylvia has the problem and he takes the role of helping her. It is very important to notice that Jeff is leaving his problem with Sylvia alone and is not introducing it as an issue (i.e. about her spending too much time with her family, etc.) He is not in a dependent position because he is telling Sylvia <u>what to do for him</u> using direct anger.

3. Sylvia: All you think about is your friends. You never think about me. Why don't you ever think about coming straight home and fixing things

3. It is very difficult to figure what Sylvia is really upset about. Eddie? About fixing things around the house? Coming home at a certain time? Sylvia's uncertainty and lack of

around the house?

clearly stating what she wants from Jeff, represents dependency. Notice that Sylvia did not directly respond to Jeff's statement. She was so angry, she did not even "hear" Jeff, yet.

4. Jeff: I understand what you are saying. But, tell me why you are saying that.

4. Jeff is using steps 3 & 4 of the process. He first tells her that he understands her (step 3) which reduces her drive to verbally attack him. It implies that Jeff is accepting her position. Then, he tells her the second time of the "3 Times Rule" (step 4) by telling her what to do for him again. This will help Sylvia to "hear" Jeff. Jeff is still using an element of "HTE." He is giving her instructions to explain what she is saying, which will keep him in control of his role in the conversation and continue to help Sylvia focus in on what she wants.

5. Sylvia: Why didn't you just come home? Why did you go over Eddie's

5. Notice the change in her response. The intensity of her anger level has decreased. She is

house?

not accusing him of anything, but still uses passive anger by questioning him.

6. Jeff: I understand what you are saying. But, this is really important to me, Sylvia. So, tell me why you are raising this issue.

6. Jeff is using steps 3 & 4 of the process, which continues to lower her need to be aggressive. Jeff stresses the importance to him of Sylvia telling him why she is raising this as an issue. Then he tells her, for the third time (of the "3 Times Rule"), to tell him why she is raising this as an issue. Notice that Jeff has not asked a single question. Jeff is in control of the situation and his role in it. This will help Sylvia to take control of herself and be more clear about what she wants.

7. Sylvia: I'm raising this issue because you don't care about me. If you did, why would you spend so much time with your friends? You could spend more time with me. How come you don't?

7. Although it may sound as if Sylvia is responding to what Jeff said to tell him, she isn't. Her issue is what she wants, not what he's not doing. This represents dependency: she has still not told Jeff what she wants. She is depending on Jeff to figure it out. Sylvia herself may not know what she wants.

Is the main issue whether Jeff cares about her or not? Notice Sylvia's accusations about Jeff not caring about her enough. Sylvia is expecting Jeff to become defensive and then she will attack his defense. But this was not her initial issue (his spending time with Eddie). Jeff is not and cannot be the problem. The problem is: Sylvia's needs are not getting met.

8. Jeff: I wonder if you want to talk about if I care about you or not. Tell me if that is what you want to talk about.

8. Jeff is using steps 5 & 2 of the process. He is determining if this issue is "8 Feet" for Sylvia. This represents step 5 of the process. Then he uses step 2 of the process, direct anger (a statement not a question), and tells her to tell him if that is what she wants to talk about. This does not impose on her "free will" and it clarifies what Jeff wants from Sylvia at this point. This precludes an argument. Notice how much more controlled and focused they are.

9. Sylvia: No. What I want to talk to you about is that we are having a surprise birthday party for my mother at her house on Friday and I want you to be there right after work. But, you spend all of your time at Eddie's. So, are you gonna go?

9. Sylvia finally begins to focus on her real problem, telling Jeff her concerns. She wants him to go to her mother's surprise birthday party and anticipated that he may be late or might not show up because of the time spent with Eddie. She was able to get to this point because Jeff used our approach and stuck to his goal: not taking on Sylvia's problem, and telling her what to do for him. Notice how Sylvia appears to be more comfortable, too.

10. Jeff: Let me think about that. Tell me what you want me to do. That's important to me.

10. Jeff is using steps 6 & 7 of the process. "Let me think about that" is a "neutralizing/transitional" statement (Step 6), allowing time to decide if he can do this for her or not. He follows this with an instruction (Step 7). This helps Sylvia feel he is interested in what she has to say and helps reduce her original feelings of passive anger.

11. Sylvia: Well, my sister and I have been planning

11. As a result of Jeff using our approach, Sylvia is more secure

this for a while. She and her husband are going to be there and my brother and his wife and kids are going to be there too. I want you there on time and right after work because it is going to be a surprise for my mother. So, don't go by Eddie's first. Come straight to my mother's house.

12. Jeff: Okay. I'll be there. I'll go straight to your mother's house after work.

and clearly communicates what she wants to Jeff. This avoids a big argument. Jeff is now more able to see the importance the real issue had to Sylvia. Notice that Sylvia finally took charge in telling Jeff how to meet her needs, as opposed to disguising these needs into a false issue. This success is directly attributed to Jeff using our approach.

12. Jeff is using step 10 of the process. He recognizes how important this issue is to Sylvia. He decided to do what she wanted, which makes her happy because she is getting what she wants. Jeff will also feel good because he is successful in pleasing Sylvia as well as himself. Jeff also got what he wanted. Because he used our approach, his problem was solved in the middle of the process. So, steps 8 and 9 were not needed. Again, if you get what you want, you don't need the rest of the process, except for the last step 10, as Jeff did.

13. Sylvia: Thank you. I love you for this.	13. Even though Sylvia is not aware of it (using our approach) she is also using step 10. This is basically an automatic response. When you get what you want, you are happy that you got what you wanted and that the other person is doing it for you.

Jeff got much better results from using the "Lewis Approach." He used it and avoided a squabble with Sylvia, which would have decreased his comfort level with her. Essentially it allowed Sylvia's behavior to change. The "Lewis Approach" completely changed the dynamics of how Sylvia felt. Jeff conveyed his acceptance, support, and understanding of Sylvia, which allowed her to feel freer to tell him clearly what she wanted from him. Basically, he told her what to do for him, using our approach.

Further, using the "Lewis Approach," Jeff automatically helped her to focus on her issue, always respecting her "free will." He focused on what he wanted by using our approach, which automatically paved the way for a solution.

One other point: Notice that Jeff's issue with Sylvia (about her spending too much time with her family) was not discussed in the above example. This was done deliberately to help you to see how to handle situations more effectively. When someone raises a problem with you, refrain from raising your issue with them. Mixing issues is never effective and may well lead to arguments. This is not to say that if you have an issue not to bring it up. Just don't mix the two issues. Keep them separate and raise your issue at another time. If someone raises an issue with you, use the "Lewis Approach" and work on that issue, as Jeff did.

Dealing With a Parent and Child Conflict

Parent-child relationships are extremely important. In this section, a "child" covers from infancy to age 12. "Children" (adolescents) in the age group between 13 and 18, require a slightly different type of interaction. The approach is generally the same, but a special understanding of teenagers is necessary to be most effective in using our approach. Dealing with both age groups will be discussed in the section.

In infancy, the main drive is basic survival (eating, sleeping, etc.). As time goes on, children begin to develop their individuality, social skills, personality, and form a foundation to transition from childhood to adolescence. During this period, it is important that the parents <u>stay</u> in the authoritative role, <u>without imposing</u> their authority on the child. If an adult does this, he or she is operating as an equal with the child, which puts the child in the adult role; a role they are not ready to handle yet. Parents must use their authority to teach their children what they need to know to function successfully in life.

Often, parents may experience their child expressing anger by resisting defiantly, being stubborn, being rebellious, etc. Look at this behavior as the child's use of anger as a <u>change agent</u>. The parent should remember this anger is not personal, but rather the child's attempt to deal with the changes they are experiencing. We encourage the parents to see this as <u>positive</u> and take this opportunity to help the child learn better life skills. Take the child's anger and guide them to use it in the most effective way. Again, the parent is the teacher to help the child see the most effective ways to live.

When a child is angry, this signals that their needs are not being met. Parents need to guide the child to use this anger and frustration to help them find out what their needs are. This provides a solid foundation to help them learn how to get these need met.

Children, extremely dependent on their parents for their basic needs, can acutely sense their parents' anxiety. When parents are anxious, their children's security is drastically threatened. Then, children will get themselves into trouble and incur their parents' anger. Interestingly, this anger feels like security to the child; conveying the parent is in control again rather than anxious. If you are anxious, reassure your child that he or she is all right and you, as parent, will handle the problem or situation.

On a personal note, in a world where communication skills are becoming more and more important, we believe that parents should not *hit* their children. Such behavior, in our minds, is an expression of the parent's insecurity and of being out of control. All of this is transferred on to the child and, thus, damages the child's self esteem and feelings of worth. We strongly believe that parents should find another alternatives to hitting their children.

Take the time to educate your children as to _what you want them to do_. One of the main roles a parent plays in a child's life is to provide guidance and teach them the most effective way to live. The child learns and internalizes the parent's values. Eventually, children will learn the proper way handle various parts of their lives.

Additionally, we believe that parents should not tell their children "no" when their children are doing things they don't want them to do. Again, parents need to educate their children as to <u>what they want them to do</u>. Saying "no" "blocks" any human being's progress, and creates anger. Anger, in both adults and children, means their needs are not being met. Although we believe it best not to say "no," we can accept telling a child "no" if the parent then guides the child to do <u>what they want them to do</u>.

Guidance is the key. If you simply tell a child "no," you block their progress, which in turn creates anger in the child. When you take the time to <u>tell</u> the child what to do, the child feels that you really care for them. They feel more loved, worthy, and can develop a solid sense of self esteem. Children can learn more and be more effective when they learn <u>what to do</u>, in a non-threatening way, as opposed to being told what <u>not</u> to do, which can be very restrictive. As you study the following example, keep these points in mind. We are confident you will begin to notice your children becoming more cooperative and learning things better. (This will work even if only <u>one</u> parent does this, as the other parent will see the effectiveness of this and do it as well.)

Background information for this example. This is a conflict between a parent and a child about 10 years of age. Tommy does not like doing his homework. He is on the local little league team, which practices frequently.

Fifth Scenario (Before - WITHOUT the approach)

Dialogue

Commentary

1. Mom: Tommy, why haven't you been doing your homework? Why aren't you doing it now?

1. Tommy's mom expresses disappointment with Tommy. She wants him to do his homework, but does not tell him that. This represents her dependency: she wants Tommy to do something without telling him.

2. Tommy: I had to go to practice today. We have a big game coming up. Don't you want me to be a good player?

2. Tommy anticipates his answer will not be accepted. So he tries to raise feelings of guilt in his mother.

3. Mom: Is that all you think about, playing baseball? If you are going to make something out of your life you are going to have to learn.

3. Mom is asking Tommy a question to try to influence him into doing his homework, but does not give Tommy directions as to what she wants him to do. She assumes Tommy is in the

mood to learn now, when he is really interested in playing baseball. This will cause Tommy to become more defensive and resist.

4. Tommy: I'm learning. Don't you want me to have fun?

4. Tommy is obviously just thinking about baseball. Again he tries to get his mother to feel guilty for attempting to "take his fun away."

5. Mom: If you don't your homework, I'm not going to let you go to practice. So, you are going to have to make up your mind.

5. Mom sees this interaction as a confrontation, but she is really turning the authority over to Tommy. ("If you don't do something, then I won't let you do this.") Tommy's next actions control what his mother will do next. If he does one thing, she must do something and if he does nothing, she still has to do something. She has the burden. But if Tommy is in control, his mother will have more anxiety which will intensify his own anxiety and increase his feelings of insecurity.

6. Tommy: No one else's mother is making their child miss practice. And Dad likes it when I practice baseball.

6. Children are experts at playing one parent against the other. He is trying to get his mother to feel guilty for expressing her passive anger. His statement makes it sound as if she is being unfair to him. She is unconsciously giving Tommy the authority, which he uses to question her motives. But Tommy hopes that his mother will take the authority back and make the decisions.

7. Mom: Well, I'm not any of the other parents. If the other parents let their children run out and play in the middle of the street and get run over by a car, do you think that I should let you run out and get hurt like that?

7. Mom is trying to reason with Tommy as if he were an adult. She is not using her authority to teach or educate her son. She is questioning him to see if he will give the answers she wants, subconsciously knowing she won't get that kind of answer. Tommy's anxiety continues to cause him to resist and rebel.

8. Tommy: You don't care about me. You don't care if I got hit by a car or not. If you

8. Tommy responds to the high-level anxiety; a result of his Mom not taking charge.

did, you wouldn't treat me this way. That's why I don't like you.

Unsure of how to handle this situation, he looks for a resolution to stop this problem. Unknowingly, his mother keeps putting pressure on him. So he becomes more hostile.

9. Mom: (She slaps Tommy's bottom) You better go to your room right now young man. Your not going to get any dinner tonight until you stop talking like that.

9. Mom is angry, frustrated, and out of control. She has struck her son, which we don't recommend, as it could be interpreted by some as a form of child abuse. Striking her son has lowered Tommy's feelings of self esteem and self worth. The person to whom Tommy looks to for help and protection is the one hurting him. Tommy's mother would feel bad that she struck her son, aware she is not handling the situation properly. She is in a power struggle with her son, which makes her feel like she is a bad mother. Two people are now miserable and unhappy.

10. Tommy: You're mean. I wish you weren't my mother. (He goes to his room, slams the door, lays on his bed, and cries).

10. Tommy obviously feels bad, that his mother does not care about him. The person who should be protecting and caring for him is now his source of pain.

11. Mom: (She yells) You spoiled brat. You're just like Uncle Harry. You'll never make anything out of your life.

11. Mom is trying to free herself of guilt for striking her son and causing him pain. (i.e., Tommy yelling and crying, etc.) She does this by blaming him for being like Uncle Harry, so she can feel justified in hurting Tommy's feelings. Notice that they are not dealing with the initial problem. Not only is Tommy not doing his homework, he is not playing baseball, nor eating, and is isolated from his family. Even though Mom knows she tried her best to be a good mother, she feels responsible and guilty for causing Tommy much pain and discomfort.

Many times parents, unknowingly, give their children the role of authority, which causes anxiety in the child, and worsens the condition. Tommy's mom thought she was instructing him to do what she wanted him to do: his homework. But what she actually did was give him a choice. When Tommy indicated he wanted to play baseball rather than do his homework, Mom continued to pressure him to choose what she wanted him to choose. When Tommy rebelled, his Mom became frustrated and intensified the pressure. As the authority figure, she was not in control of the situation. The more pressure she applied the more he resisted, which ultimately lead to her striking Tommy. When he went to his room, she felt bad for causing him such pain. Mom ended up in a losing situation.

This was a truly "lose-lose" situation where nobody got what they wanted. Because of the dynamics of the discussion, they did not even get a chance to discuss this. Mom did not take the authoritative role: guiding Tommy to do what she wanted him to do. Instead, she treated him like an adult, giving him choices that Tommy, the child, could not make. But when he chose the option she _did not want_ him to do, she punished him.

Using the "Lewis Approach," let's see how Tommy's mother, under the same circumstances, gets totally different (positive) results with her son Tommy.

Fifth Scenario (After - WITH the approach)

Dialogue

1. Mom: Tommy, I understand you have not been doing your homework. So, every evening when you come home from school, do your homework.

2. Tommy: I have to practice baseball. Don't you want me to be a good player? I don't have to do my homework. I learned that stuff already.

3. Mom: I can understand how important baseball is to you and I know that you want to be a good player. But Tommy, I want you to do your homework to learn your lessons in school and get good grades. So, when you come home from school, do your homework assignments.

Commentary

1. Mom is using steps 1 & 2 of the process, clarifying the problem and telling him very clearly what do for her. She is giving Tommy a very clear message.

2. Tommy is resisting doing his homework because he is into playing baseball, his main focus in life right now. Also, he is trying to make his mother feel guilty.

3. Mom is using steps 3 & 4 of the process. She first tells him that she understands (step 3). This will reduce Tommy's drive to resist Mom. Then, she stresses the importance to her of Tommy doing his homework and immediately follows up by telling him a second time (Step 4 and the second of the "3 Times

Rule") what she wants him to do. Note: Mom never answered Tommy's question, which would have given him control of the conversation. She maintained her position of authority, without abusing it, and very clearly instructed Tommy again what she wanted him to do for her. By Mom keeping the controls and authority, it provided reassurance and security for Tommy.

4. Tommy: None of the other kids have to do their homework. They get to play as long as they want to. Their parents don't nag them. Besides Dad likes it when I practice baseball. How come I have to do my homework?

4. Tommy is attempting to play "one parent against another" by telling Mom that none of the other kids parents are concerned about homework. Tommy also points out that even Dad likes when he practices baseball. Tommy is trying to imply that Mom is not a good mother because she is asking him to do his homework. He is also trying to make her feel guilty by implying that she is nagging

him and being unfair. He is attempting to act as an authority and question her judgment. (Realistically, he wants to accept her authority but he also wants his way).

5. Mom: I understand that some parents may not expect their children to do their homework and I can understand how you feel. But Tommy, I want you to do your homework. I want you to learn and get good grades. Even though some children may not do their homework, when you come home from school, do it the way I want you to and do your homework. Do the best you can with your homework, and if you have problems, let me know.

5. Mom is using steps 3 & 4 of the process. She does not agree, disagree, or determine whether he is right or wrong. This would put Tommy in the position of authority. He is raising the issue about other parents to strengthen his position. If she deals with that other issue, she would be on Tommy's topic, not her own. Instead, she tells him that she understands what he is saying. Then, Mom uses step 4 (i.e. the third of the "3 Times Rule") by giving Tommy very clear and detailed instructions. She tells him to do his homework and if he needs help to let her know. She drives this point home using

271

direct anger and tells Tommy exactly what to do for her. Her message is also very instructional and supportive.

6. Tommy: I don't want to do that stupid old homework anyway. It's boring.

6. Tommy, still resisting, challenges whether the homework is important. But notice Tommy's tone is much different. Tommy is almost ready to do the homework. He makes a final effort of resisting before he does what his mother wants him to do.

7. Mom: It may be boring to you and I know what it felt like to me when I was your age. It seemed boring to me, too. But Tommy, I want you to learn to do the work anyway even though it may seem boring. So, do your homework each day. It is important to me that you do it.

7. Mom is using steps 5, 6, & 7 of the process. Step 5 acknowledges to Tommy that homework may be boring, in comparison to playing baseball, and this could represent "8 Feet" for him (i.e. why he doesn't want to do his homework). She uses a form of step 6, a neutralizing/transitional statement, by telling him that she remembers how she felt about her homework as

a youngster. This helps to reduce Tommy's resistance. Then she immediately uses step 7, using more direct anger by clearly telling Tommy what she wants him to do for her.

8. Tommy: Well, could I get a new baseball batting glove if I do my homework?

8. Tommy, in his own way, is acknowledging that he is going to do his homework. It may sound as if he is trying to negotiate but he is not. He is only trying to "save face." It's his way of transitioning from resisting to going along. It is very important for Mom to recognize that Tommy is going along with her rather than talking about the batting glove and shift the discussion. This would give Tommy authority equal to hers. Mom would then have to start this process all over again.

9. Mom: *Tommy*, (said with "kindly" emphasis) don't ask me if you can have a batting

9. Mom is using steps 8 & 9 of the process. By Mom saying Tommy's name with

glove. Doing your homework is important to me. So, tell me that you are going to do your homework. I'd really feel a lot better about that.

"kindly" emphasis (indicated by italics), she is utilizing the guilt that Tommy would have as a result of his using passive anger and his resisting her. Mom uses step 9 of the process by being more selfish (positive selfishness). She is very specific about what she is telling him to do for her, which makes it easier for Tommy to go along. It helps him move from a state of resistance to a state of compliance. The instructions Mom gives Tommy are clear, direct, and easy to understand. They empower him to act. Notice also how Mom has not threatened, challenged, or tried to use force to get him to do his homework.

10. Tommy: *Okay*, (said reluctantly), I'll do it. But, I still won't like it.

10. Tommy has finally overcome his own resistance, as a result of Mom using our approach. He has worked through his resistance of doing his

homework. He says "I won't like it" to see if Mom will respond to that comment. If she does, it could extend the conversation and refuel his resistance.

11. Mom: Tommy, I am happy you are going along with me and accepting doing your homework. Doing your homework is important to me and I am glad that you understand.

11. Mom is using step 10 of the process. She got what she wanted and has rewarded Tommy. This allows Mom to recognize and acknowledge that she got what she wanted. It also lets Tommy know that he has pleased his Mom, so he will feel good. Furthermore, it prevents them from getting back into this conversation because both will recognize that the issue is completed and they have come to a resolution. Notice how Mom did not respond to Tommy's: "I won't like it". She is focused on her issue. Mom must allow Tommy to have the "free will" to like it or not. If she responded to that comment

and tried to make him <u>like</u> his homework as well, Tommy would view this as his Mom trying to control or force him. This would renew his motivation to resist and cause Mom more trouble. But Mom stuck with our approach and got <u>what she wanted with words</u>.

See how much better and successful the dialog between Tommy and his Mom went when she used the "Lewis Approach." She stayed fully focused on what <u>she</u> wanted, even when Tommy tried to manipulate her into losing that focus. She used <u>direct anger</u> to provide clear guidance and instruction as to what she wanted him to do for her. Mom also maintained her role of authority, but never tried to persuade, force, threaten, or strike Tommy. She also respected Tommy's "free will."

Mom used the "Lewis Approach," which resulted in Tommy doing his homework, playing baseball, and both Mom and Tommy feeling good about the situation. They each felt successful. Perhaps most importantly in this parent-child situation, it prepares Tommy to develop effective problem-solving skills to use as he matures.

Dealing With Adolescents

As stated at the outset of this section, dealing with adolescents is slightly different from dealing with children age 12 and under. Adolescence is the most difficult time in a person's life, with so many drastic changes, physically, mentally, and spiritually. Teens also have somewhat different issues and needs than do children age 12 and under.

During the transition period from child to adult, teens need to develop new decision-making skills. They are moving from having "all" of the decisions made for them to having to make "all" of the decisions for themselves when they become adults. This is initially a difficult and monumental task. Decisions made by their parents when they were children were more focused, clear, and definite. Teenagers have to start making decisions on their own: what clothes to wear; which friends to spend time, what foods to eat; what goals to aim in the future, etc. These are tough and challenging decisions for teens. And not making a decision is also a decision.

Young adults often feel alone and very insecure, as they struggle to feel a sense of belonging with their peers. Although their facade may be tough, inside they are unsure and afraid. Many times, teens will do things they don't want to do simply to "fit in" with their peers, of whom they might be afraid. These teens often find comfort in "clicks" and groups. Many turn to gangs as well. Today, the teen suicide rate is higher than in past years, a clear result of increased pressure, due to the complex world in which we live.

One key issue to emphasize: teenagers _need guidance from their parents and other adults_. Whether they know this or not, they _want_ this guidance. They prefer to be dependent on their parents, but they can't be anymore. They must learn how to develop independent "living" skills in order to cope in the world and share that independence with others. Parents and other adults begin to turn the decision-making processes over to the teenagers. The inability of these teens to develop effective decision-making skills is often the reason behind school dropouts, joining gangs, having emotional breakdowns, and even suicide.

Through the teenagers transition phase, the parent must remain in the authoritative role, and maintain family values. Parents need to aid in helping teenagers make their own decisions, but remain in a position of authority and determine if the teen is making the best decision for him or her self. The parents need to consider what the family values are to determine if the teen's ultimate decision will be harmful to him or her. Then, the parents must help teenagers determine and understand the consequences of their decisions, both positive and negative. This provides the proper guidance and instruction to help adolescents develop more solid decision-making skills as they enter adulthood.

Let us look at an example. Say you had a 16-year-old teenage boy who wanted to drop out of school to become a race-car driver. But the rest of the family had gone to colleges and universities with professional careers in mind. Clearly the 16 year old's values differed from the rest of the family. The parent would want to understand the teen's need to become a race car driver. The parent could do this by using a modified version of "HTE" (Have Them Explain): Sit and talk with the adolescent, have him tell about his desire, goals, etc. During this discussion, the parent may want to influence the teenager to make a decision more consistent with the family values, encouraging him to pursue a career that would be best for the teenager.

This may stifle the creativity of certain young individuals. What if the parents of some of the great entertainers of the world had discouraged them from entering the difficult and competitive entertainment field? Or what if the parents of great sports heroes told them that professional sports was too risky and they should finish college instead? Our world would be different than it is today. The main point is that teenagers need guidance to make these type of decisions, and parents play a pivotal role in helping teens develop their best decision-making skills. Keep in mind, however, that teenagers also must be allowed their "free will" to make their own final decisions. Teenagers will either use your suggestions or "follow their dream," be it success or failure. But, again, it's important for parents to provide the _foundation_ and _backbone_ to help guide their teens to acquire and develop effective and sound decision-making skills to the very best of their ability.

279

The following is a brief "mini-dialogue" example of how the "Lewis Approach" can be used in dealing with a teenager.

Note: Unlike all of the other examples in this section, we are only showing how the parent uses the "Lewis Approach" to help their teenager through a particular situation. We are only illustrating the "how to do it" section for this scenario.

Tommy, 17 years of age, is considering not to attend college after he graduates from high school, unlike his older brother and sister who both went to universities. His mind seems to be set on working at an auto body shop, where some older friends of his work. Mom is concerned. Tommy gets goods grades in school and college seems like the next natural step for him. She is puzzled as to why he is considering the auto body shop and wants to find out more about that.

Scenario (WITH the approach)

Dialogue

Commentary

1. Mom: Tommy, I understand that you do not want to go to college after you graduate from high school and that you want to work at an auto body shop instead. Tell me if that is what you want to do.

1. Mom is using a form of steps 1 & 2 of the process. Step 1 seeks clarification from Tommy so that she can identify what she wants from him. Notice she does not ask questions. This allows for free communication. Tommy

is not being confronted, only directed to contribute to a conversation. Mom is using step 2 by expecting Tommy to resist. She has phrased her statement to prepare herself for resistance. She approaches it objectively in a non-confrontational way. Yet, the topic is still direct.

2. Tommy: Yeah. I don't want to go to college. That takes too long. I just want to get myself a good job. Besides, my friends work at the auto body shop and they like it a lot. The cars are real cool.

2. Tommy appears to be vague as to what he wants to do. He is expressing that he wants to avoid college to work at an auto body shop. Based on the way he is presenting his situation, Mom can see that what he is saying is not consistent with the family values. This would help Mom to reinforce these family values to Tommy rather than confront his decision about working at the body shop.

3. Mom: I understand what you are saying but let's talk about that. I wonder if you knew that your father and I

3. Mom is using steps 3 and 4 of the process. Telling him she understands, reduces Tommy's resistance and

want you to go to college. Tell me if you knew that.

makes him more receptive to what she wants him to do. Mom again clarifies what she wants, but in a way that instructs what she wants from him. This is the reinforcement of the family value system and goal. Mom the uses step 4. She uses direct anger ("tell me if you knew that.") This helps to register this message in Tommy's mind and helps him to respond. He also sees that his mother is willing to listen and that what he has to say is important to her.

4. Tommy: Kind of. But, I don't want to go to college. I don't know what I want to do anyway. Besides, I can make a career out of auto body work. There are a lot of cars out there that need body work.

4. Again, Tommy is vague about his decision, which doesn't seem well thought out. There is no goal; long term or realistic. He is also not following the family value structure, which can serve as a good guide for Mom in her determining the reality of what he wants to do.

5. Mom: Tommy, I didn't know you felt that way. But, it is important to me that you go to college. What your father and I want is for all of the children to get a good education and we want you to get a good education, too. Tell me if there is anything keeping you from doing that.

5. Mom is using steps 3 & 5 of the process. She first uses step 3 ("I didn't know you felt that way.") This lets Tommy know that she understands what he said. Mom then uses step 5, asking Tommy to tell her what is getting in his way. This is to evaluate whether Tommy has the emotional readiness to go to college and to identify what barriers he faces (Notice that Mom did not use all three parts of the "3 Times Rule." She is not yet definite as to what she wants Tommy to do. She is still in a problem-solving mode that will allow her to decide what she wants. When she decides, she can then utilize all three parts of the "3 Times Rule.")

6. Tommy: College is a waste of time. I'll never get to use the stuff they'd teach me in college anyway. Everybody says that.

6. Tommy is trying to find a way to resist going to college; it's his way of questioning the uncertainties of life. Subconsciously he is asking Mom for support and guidance. He is essentially

saying to Mom, "Is this true?"

7. Mom: I understand that there may be some people who feel that way and this can be very confusing. But a college education prepares you for the future and gives you good decision making ability. It is important to me that you get this opportunity to develop this.
So, make education a value to you and go to college.

7. Mom is using steps 3 & 7 of the process. Mom uses step 3 by telling Tommy, again, that she understands what he is saying. This allows him to be more understanding of her and eliminates his feelings of being criticized. She is also acknowledging his viewpoint, an effective step to use. Mom uses step 7 by telling Tommy what she wants, and the importance it has to her. She addresses his concern about whether college has value, reinforces that it does, and that it is especially valuable to the family. She is instructing him to make education a value to him, which is direct anger, and makes it very clear as to what she wants him to do.

8. Tommy: You and Dad are trying to run my life. You think you know what is best for me. But, only I know what is best for me.

8. Tommy may sound tough, but this is his near final attempt at resisting. He hopes Mom will get upset with him, which would justify his continued rebellion. If she did get upset, he would have been successful in changing the topic. Mom recognizes that Tommy is very close to going along with her and sticks to using direct anger statements to tell Tommy how to please her.

9. Mom: *Tommy* (said with emphasis like she is irritated), show more respect when you talk to me. I understand how difficult it may be to make the decision about going to college and I understand how you feel. But, to go to college. Do it my way. That would really make me feel good.

9. Mom is using steps 8, 3, & 9 of the process. Mom uses step 8 by saying Tommy's name in a way that shows he has hurt her feelings. This utilizes the guilt Tommy would naturally have as a result of his being rude (i.e. using passive anger). This will reduce Tommy's drive to continue being rude or aggressive. Telling him to be more respectful is a direct anger phrase, which gives Tommy instructions as to

what to do and how to please her. This helps Tommy <u>focus</u> on what Mom is saying, making it easier to go along with her. (This also helps teens to control their impulses, reduces their feelings of insecurity, and provides them with better problem solving skills at home and elsewhere). Mom then uses step 3; she understands what he is saying. This tells him he is free to talk and that he is heard. Mom then uses step 9 (by telling him to go to college, etc.) She immediately follows that up by telling him <u>to do it her way</u>.

10. Tommy: My friends said they could almost guarantee getting me a job at the body shop after I graduate from high school. I've been going down there on weekends already.

10. This is Tommy's "last gasp" to test Mom's sincerity. (Surprisingly, many parents give up at this point and cave in to their teenager's resistance when they are so close to a resolution.) But Mom recognizes how close she is to getting Tommy to go along with her.

11. Mom: That sounds really good and I can see why you are happy about that. But, even though it sounds good, I would be happy with you going to college and getting a good education. That's what I want for you. So Tommy, plan on attending college.

11. Mom is using steps 3 & 9 of the process. She first uses step 3 (giving him credit for the work he has done.) Then Mom uses step 9 (telling Tommy how important a good education is to her, etc.) Mom follows this using direct anger: Telling Tommy to plan on attending college. She repeats this to clarify what she wants , thereby, making it easier for Tommy to go along with her.

12. Tommy: Okay, I'll go. I guess it may be fun. Some of my other friends are going to State College. Maybe I could go there with them.

12. With Mom's help, and how she used our approach in this book, Tommy has worked through his resistance in going to college. He has also learned decision-making skills, which are very important to the development of his preparation for life as an adult.

13. Mom: Good Tommy. That sounds great. I am very happy and glad that you are

13. Mom has used step 10 of the process. She first rewards Tommy; letting him know

going to college.

that he just pleased her and made her happy. This also acknowledges that Mom got what she wanted. Tommy feels good too because he has pleased his Mom. People like having the ability to please others. Using step 10 also reduces any remaining feelings of guilt that Mom may have as a result of using direct anger to get what she wanted. The process is successfully complete.

Mom used the "Lewis Approach" to help Tommy fulfill the family values of education, which are important to her. This type of conversation could have turned into a big argument, where neither would have felt happy with the other or themselves. But thanks to Mom following our approach, she got what she wanted. Tommy eventually went along with her out of his own "free will."

Aware of dealing with an adolescent son, she understood the crucial time in his life and helped him with the decision-making process. By using the family values as a guideline, she stayed focused on the decision-making process to help Tommy arrive at a sound decision. She was also able to weigh his sincerity as to what he wanted to do and then helped him develop problem-solving skills by using this process. Tommy will now be able to draw on this experience in future decision-making efforts.

Summary and Conclusion

This book is designed to help you solve problems now, and to avoid countless hours seeking unproductive advice from friends, or even professionals. We know that all of us encounter problems with others from time to time: best friends, parents, spouses, boyfriends, girlfriends, children's, acquaintances, even strangers. We have found that when people experience difficulties in dealing with others, they often lack a consistent or effective way to handle them.

Through the years, we have observed people try to improvise, using reason, logic, coercion, or any method they think will work, including manipulation - though this may not be intentional. But we have seen this can create arguments, disagreements, and other painful conversations, which often leave both people unhappy or dissatisfied with one another, without knowing why they failed to get what they wanted.

This book is designed to help you recognize, specifically and with greater clarity, *what you want*. Then, we give you the specific skills and tools to get what you want, no matter with whom you are dealing. Using the "Lewis Approach," you will automatically be more loved by other person. However, this book *does not try to change you or the other person*. Instead, it provides you with an effective way to help people do or give you what you want without either of you having to change. The process described in this book is based on the innate desire of people to please others. Using our approach, you <u>tell the person what to do or how to please you</u>. As we have shown and emphasized throughout, the process <u>empowers</u> people with the ability and "free will" desire to please.

Summary of Essential Ground Rules

There are a few relatively simple things to keep in mind when using the "Lewis Approach." Firstly, "see yourself as perfect the way you are." This does not necessarily mean that you are right or wrong. Only that you are <u>you</u>, unique, one of a kind. You are a perfect <u>you</u>. Secondly, use "positive selfishness" and demonstrate "loving yourself." This means you focus only on your needs and wanting everything your way, but never at the other person's expense. Also let other people "use positive selfishness" as well.

Summary of Anger - A New View of Anger

The most important part of the "Lewis Approach" involves the use of "anger." Anger is the key element which drives the process. We offered a new and different way of looking at anger as a change agent, a vehicle to help you get your needs met. We discussed the use of "passive anger" (negative and ineffective) and "direct anger" (positive and effective).

The other important point was the "value of being independent" - (i.e., knowing what you want and taking *control* of getting what you want). This will keep you from being dependent.

Summary of Getting Through Resistance

Another helpful principle discussed was "analyzing the other person as well as yourself." This means "not taking on the other person's problem" and remaining objective in order to understand the other person and his or her intentions. The "8 Feet Rule" and the use of "I" and "You" words are key principles that help you to know what the person is capable of doing, and when one is simply resisting. We also discussed how to overcome resistance, which included using "understanding / positive acknowledgment" statements, "being as clear as you can be about what you want," allowing people to maintain their "free will", and using the "3 Times Rule." Getting though resistance also included being "subjective in an objective way" and "utilizing guilt" effectively. We also illustrated a number of specific "key phrases" that you can use to help you get through a person's resistance. To conclude the process, we talked about "how to know when you got what you wanted."

Summary of Staying Focused

The section entitled "Getting Out of Trouble - The Life Raft," focused on how to help you regain <u>control</u> of your emotions and get "back on track." That section also discussed "Troubleshooting ;" When you think you are using our approach, but are not getting the results you want. We included a checklist to help you determine where your breakdown is and how to get re-focused on getting what you want. This section illustrated "The Process" of how our approach, step by step, works encompassing all of the skills and tools we taught throughout the book.

Summary of Comprehensive Examples

This section gave you "before" and "after" examples of how to use the steps of "The Process" to get what you want. Five examples covered some of the more typical interactions that people get into. But our approach and words can be used in virtually any situation you encounter. You can actually take the "after" or positive examples and use the actual words as written and achieve the same effective results illustrated in the examples. We felt that this format (i.e., examples of "before" and "after") really helps you see how the process works, phrase by phrase, to make it as easy as possible to do and achieve positive results with people in virtually any situation.

Remember, this book is designed to: 1. Help you get your needs met more easily and much more often. 2. Instantly improve your personal and professional relationships. 3. Help you be more in control of the things that happen to you with people. 4. Help you be more in control of your life.

Conclusion

Using the "Lewis Approach" will help you to feel better about yourself, and others will automatically feel better about you. They won't know why, but _you_ will. And you will always have our approach with you in this book. Use it when you need it, and watch your quality of life improve. Enjoy yourself and live a happier life!

Bibliography

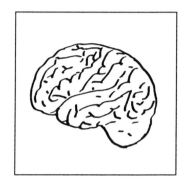

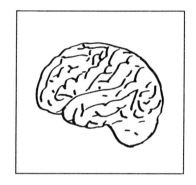

Chuck's Brain   Charles' Brain

Chuck and Charles co-authored this book exclusively. All of the concepts and applications documented as part of the "Lewis Approach" were either devised and/or created over the years through experiences realized by Chuck or Charles. While a few of the concepts may sound like or be similar to those expressed in other books, no sources, written or otherwise, were consulted or used as reference by Chuck or Charles during the writing.

Glossary

"3 Times Rule" - Tell what you want others to do for you up to three separate times. You direct your issue toward the person to ensure their attention and that they are hearing you. The first time they may be dwelling on their own thoughts and not really hearing you, (i.e. the words did not register in their brain). The second time, they may only hear part of what you said. The third time, (here you may start by saying their name first) you will have the person's full attention. They have "heard" your message and it has registered in their brain. The "Three Times Rule" thus helps the person to do what you want them to do.

"8 Foot Rule" - Jumping "8 Feet" is analogous to the track meet high-jump event. To recognize when you ask a person to do something that they cannot do. When you direct others to give you what you want with words, sometimes people will not do so -- at first or at all. Why? The request may be beyond their capacity. This represents "8 Feet" for the other person. To help the other person "jump 8 feet" and please you, empower them: giving them your strength by using "Positive Selfishness" and by "Tapping into the person's desire to please." This will help the person give you as much as they can, possibly even clearing the "8 Feet" -- which may exceed your needs.

Anger - a change agent. The only emotion that brings about change in interactions between people. Results when a person's needs are not being met or when their progress is blocked. Is the internal motivation to get those needs met or to resume progress.

Anger Is Like Money - Direct anger is like using real money to get what you want from people. In direct anger, you take responsibility for telling others what to do for you, which creates a sense of value for you. By contrast, passive anger is like using a counterfeit money -- nothing of value is received -- and you may get deeper into trouble. Your needs do not get met.

Dependent - To want, need, or expect something from someone without directly communicating your expectations. (This implies expecting others to be "mind readers.") You are dependent when you use passive anger.

Direct Anger - A positive force. Using instructional statements with people that begin with action words (verbs) to instruct them how to please you and to meet your needs. Action words (verbs) include: Let, Do, Take, Give, Work, Arrange, etc. These words take responsibility for communicating to a person exactly what you want and instructs them to give that to you. You focus only on your needs. Direct Anger is the primary and an essential tool to get what you want with words. It gives clear and concise instructions on how to please you. Direct anger is a change agent: it effects changes that you want -- i.e. getting your needs met.

Don't Take On Someone Else's Problem - Occurs when someone accuses, blames, or pressures you about what you may or may not have done. You take on other people's problem when you become defensive, explain your position, or become actively involved with the solution to their problem. You also take on others' problems when you feel generally negative -- i.e. you feel bad, unhappy, or uncomfortable, as a result of others' behavior. Generally, you know you have taken on another person's problem when you first approach someone in a relatively pleasant mood and leave in an unpleasant mood -- i.e. feeling uncomfortable, defensive, etc.

"Free Will" - Allows the person the freedom to accept or refuse what you are telling them to do. Respects people's freedom to choose whether they can do what you want. However, you do not give the person a choice as to what <u>you</u> want. You respect their decision to say yes or no. But you only give them one choice: what to do to meet your needs. If they resist, continue with the process to help the person overcome their resistance. This approach respects their intrinsic "free will" -- you are <u>influencing</u> their choice without controlling it.

Guilt - When a person feels that they have done something wrong, bad, or have hurt or offended someone. Whenever you express any anger, you will experience guilt. This is automatic. When expressing Direct Anger, this guilt will be minimal because it is a more loving expression, both to the giver and receiver. But, guilt feelings will be significantly heavier when you express Passive Anger because it is painful to the person expressing and the person receiving. This results in a "pool of guilt" which can be tapped into to protect yourself from another's release of Passive Anger toward you. It can also be utilized to help reduce another's resistance in meeting your needs.

"HTE" (Have Them Explain) - An acronym for "Have Them Explain". "HTE" is a direct anger statement which instructs others to explain the rationale behind what they say. Used primarily when you feel pressured -- when someone is rude, accusatory, verbally attacks, blames, questions, or coerces you. "HTE" helps people to focus on the issue or problem, creating a harmonious climate. This helps the person with the problem to seek a solution, as opposed to "dumping" problems on others. The use of "HTE" helps others feel your concern and care for your issue. They feel disinclined to continue verbal attacks or to "dump" their problem on you.

"I" Words - Used in conversation, they are healthy indicators to help you determine the intent of the other person and helps guide you to an effective response. "I" words express sharing, caring, sincerity, and clarity -- all attempts to be closer emotionally. "I" words also reveal the inner thinking of the other person. Those who use "I" words are more open and willing to have their views scrutinized. Used as a determinant of what others are really saying. This will help guide you in your responses.

Independent - To decide what you want, to focus only on your needs, and to communicate those needs to others and tell them how they can meet those needs for you. Independence is self-empowering. You take charge of getting your needs met. You are independent when you use direct anger.

Love Yourself - See Positive Selfishness.

Negative Selfishness - Thinking of your needs at the other person's expense. Being selfish by being competitive, practicing one-upmanship, or preventing someone from getting what they want in order to get what you want first. Often, such selfishness involves manipulation, coercion, confrontation, and the like.

One Anger At A Time - Using only one anger at a time: direct anger, a sign of independence. This one anger conveys what you want done, how you want that done, and to execute that for you. Using more than one anger -- such as raising your voice, pointing your finger, pounding the table, etc., and using direct anger, represents dependency and reduces the power inherent in direct anger.

Passive (Indirect) Anger - A negative force. When you expect something from someone (i.e. doing, saying, believing, etc.) without <u>telling</u> or giving them clear instructions on how to do it. This type of anger arises from a very dependent and weak position. How to identify passive anger: When people are critical, complain, yell, raise their voice, are violent, sarcastic, blame, manipulate, coerce, question, accuse, or other similar negative behaviors. Those who use passive anger do <u>not</u> take responsibility for getting their needs met. Passive anger only creates hurt, confusion, pain, etc. All in all, a very difficult and self-defeating way to communicate.

Positive Acknowledgment - When you use positive words to give the other person credit, to influence their reaction to you, and have them respond in a more pleasing way. Positive acknowledgment shows that your respect the person's opinion or view point, even if you don't particularly like what they have said. Positive acknowledgment is designed to influence the other person to shift from being critical or judgmental with you to being more positive and accepting of you. It automatically reduces or eliminates their need to resist you. Additionally, it disarms the other person, in a non-confrontational way; they feel accepted, heard, understood, and appreciated by you.

Positive Selfishness - Thinking of your needs and getting those needs met, but not at another's expense. Positive selfishness does not consider the needs of the other person. That is their responsibility. Leave that part to them. However, <u>do not force</u> others to do anything. Instead, you clarify and direct others as to how <u>you</u> want things done. This concept enhances social interaction and reduces conflict. Positive selfishness is the healthy vehicle which allows you to love yourself.

Programming People ("Avoid Programming People") - An irrational attempt to force or coerce others to respond in a specific way in certain situations; then depend on them to behave or react accordingly every time. This ignores and disrespects others own needs, wants, and feelings. Essentially, this concept is like you trying to program someone as you would a computer -- and at the other person's expense of not getting their own needs met. Attempts to rob others of their "free will."

See Yourself As Perfect The Way You Are - All the good about you is perfect, all the bad is perfect, all your mistakes are perfect. In short, you are perfect being you. This concept is powerful: it enables you to focus attention on what others say to you instead of focusing on your faults. You are then in a good position to use Direct Anger to get your needs met. Note: You also see the other person as perfect the way they are.

Subjective In An Objective Way - You present your story, which is subjective because it is from your perspective, in an <u>objective</u> way -- which means you are focused on the facts or issues involved, free of personal distortions: emotions, feelings, prejudices, etc. You zero in on the facts that emphasize your point of view. Being subjective in an objective way allows others to better trust what you say and be more willing to do things for you. Think only of your needs and let others worry about theirs. Simultaneously, you must be objective in how you present your subjective or personal view. To do this, you eliminate your strong emotional feelings from the way you deliver your viewpoint. Present the facts of your personal viewpoint in an objective light. This concept is particularly effective in influencing others to see things from your perspective and go along more freely. Being subjective in an objective way reduces or eliminates the chances of the person's resistance.

Tapping Into A Person's Desire To Please - The use of specific words to stimulate a person's innate desire and motivation to please and be successful with others. These words convey how they would please you, satisfy you, make you happy, and be a success with you doing what you want them to do. A sense of success awakens self-gratification and empowerment. Hence, people have the ability to please themselves by pleasing you.

Understanding - Tells others that you understand what they are communicating to you. This does not necessarily mean you <u>understand</u> or agree with the substance of what they are saying. It simply means that you <u>understand</u> their words. Understanding helps others to feel accepted and reduces the need to force ideas on you. It gives the person the feeling that they have conveyed their message to you; that you <u>listened</u>. This allows them to be more open and accepting of what <u>you</u> have to say -- which makes it easier for the person to go along with you.

"You" Words - When you hear or use the word "you" in conversation, they are indicators of the person's insecurity and conveys emotional distancing, un-involvement, and separation. They are also very judgmental and put the receiver of the "you" words on the spot. "You" words are almost always used when blaming others, being confrontational, being judgmental, or in negative conversational situations. As with "I" words, used as a determinant of what others are really saying. This will help guide you in your responses.

Index

A

communication, 38, 43, 67
     non-communication, 40
conflicts, eliminate by positive selfishness, 33-34
control, 67, 293
controlling others, 73
coping skills, 130
courtroom scenario, 74
criticism, 37, 54, 64, 123, 199, 212

D

decision, making a, 31
decision-making skills, 277, 278, 279
denial, 39
dependency, 45, 49, 52, 55, 65, 66, 77, 86-89, 96-98,   123,
     150, 172, 200, 210, 212, 215, 217, 229, 238,   244, 245, 48,
250, 252, 253, 254, 263, 297
     definition of, 87
     roots of, 89-90
desire to be successful, 136
desire to please, tapping into a person's, 136-138, 304
direct anger, See anger.
     statements, 96, 105, 119
directions, giving, 54
discussion, blaming, 122
doing something for you, 165-167
Don and Keith,
     with Lewis Approach, 233-241
     without Lewis Approach, 226-232

don't take on another person's problem, 102-109, 125, 188, 241, 252, 256, 292, 298

E

8 feet rule, 110-119, 182, 187, 189, 190, 206, 218, 225, 237, 255, 272, 292, 296
emotional money, 60, 61
emotions, 118
empowering others, 46, 48, 67

F

family value system, 282
fear of heights, 18
focus, don't shift, 117-118
four-step process, 192-194
free will, 29, 46, 47, 56, 65, 98, 115, 117, 140-141, 145, 157, 178, 180, 184, 187, 204, 205, 207, 212, 215, 221, 225, 239, 255, 258, 275, 276, 288, 292, 298

G

gratification, 136
ground rules, 187-188, 291
guidance, 262
guilt, 52, 53, 64, 100, 190, 192, 193, 198, 200, 202, 207, 215, 218-220, 232, 238, 240, 249, 250, 263-265, 267, 269, 270, 274, 285, 299

K

L

M

situations affect their, 101

N

needs,
> getting your needs met, 29
> specific, 27

negative selfishness, 104, 145, 300
negative words, 69, 70
negatives, don't point out your own, 32
neutralizing/transition phrases, 162-164, 190, 256, 272
non-communication, 40

O

one anger at a time, 178, 183, 211, 224, 301

P

parent-child relationships, 260-262
passive
> aggression, 190
> anger, 39-44, 57, 60, 66, 84, 105, 123, 147, 148,
> 177, 178, 193, 199-202, 206, 210-211, 213,
> 217-219, 226, 227, 229-232, 234, 237-240,
> 247, 249, 254, 256, 265, 274, 285, 297, 299,
> 301
> hostility, 80
> resistance, 148, 149
> verb, 123

Q

R

S

T

About the Authors

Before creating the "Lewis Approach," Chuck had accumulated over three decades of experience as a psychotherapist and clinical social worker. He began his professional work in 1961 as a psychiatric technician at the Neuropsychiatric Institute at the University of California at Los Angeles. Later, as a psychiatric social worker at Metropolitan State Hospital in Norwalk, California, he studied psychoanalysis with Dr. Rudolph Eckstein.

From that point forward, Chuck began to develop his own unique approach which eventually evolved into the writing of this book.

As Supervisor and Team Leader of a multidisciplinary staff at a mental health clinic in Los Angeles, Chuck continued to develop his "healing" approach and therapeutic skills in helping people solve their problems with others. His approach proved extremely beneficial in his sessions with clients. He successfully accelerated the resolution of their problems. Encouraged by his success, colleagues began to send their most difficult patients to him.

Chuck has taught "the basics" of his approach at numerous psychiatric clinics and community agencies in the Greater Los Angeles area.

Chuck has since shifted the focus of his practice toward everyday people with everyday problems and conflicts, although he still enjoys working with those with more involved issues.

Most recently, Chuck, with his son Charles, has started a consulting practice featuring the "Lewis Approach" helping others to help themselves with problems, situations or conflicts they may have with others.

Charles began to use his father's approach (which had yet to be formulated) as a young teenager. (Once, he used it to enroll himself in a high school English class that he was told was full!)

Over the past several years, Charles has intensified the practice of this unique approach (which he coined the "Lewis Approach") in a variety of relationship situations at home and at work, with relatives and friends. Charles quickly learned the concepts of the approach; since being called "a master of the "Lewis Approach"" by his father, Chuck. He then began to expand on them: creating new principles and key phrases. Through his focused and diligent application, he has refined and polished the "Lewis Approach."

Besides being able to use the "Lewis Approach" successfully in situations he may encounter, Charles is also a very effective teacher of the approach. He has been sought out by friends and others to help them with their problems and situations with people. He has successfully helped family members with their relationships, friends and others with situations they have encountered with people, and provided consultation with a Priest at a local parish regarding couples with marital problems. As with his father Chuck, Charles takes great pride in teaching the "Lewis Approach" to help ensure others achieve the positive results they want.

When not providing consulting services teaching the "Lewis Approach," Chuck and Charles remain active. Chuck enjoys singing, telling jokes, and dabbling with magic tricks. He also travels to various California resort sites with his wife. Charles, a "retired" C.P.A., enjoys playing golf and other outdoor sports. His biggest joy is spending time in his new home with his wife and young son Justin.

Lewis Personal Consultants (LPC) is a recently established consulting company founded by Chuck Lewis and Charles Lewis. They combine for over 30 years of experience in changing peoples lives through confidence building, improving self image and enabling positive problem resolution skills; all resulting from the "Lewis Approach."

Both Chuck and Charles firmly believe their success is measured by your success, which gives them satisfaction for the services they provide. They are patient and understanding and help you every step of the way while learning their easy approach. Their primary focus is to get you through your problem, conflict, or situation as quickly and as easily as possible, helping you get to the important things in your life and enjoying them.

Chuck and Charles are now available to you for consultation. They offer hourly consultations in group, by couple, or individually; either in person or by phone. They are also available, by exclusive engagement, to visit your home or office and help you get results using the "Lewis Approach." Seminars are done periodically and can be arranged to your convenience.

A tapes series, including "book on tape" and "The "Lewis Approach": in action during live conversation," is also in production.

Plans for the book and tapes to be produced on computer media (i.e., CD-ROM, etc.) are currently underway and will be available in the near future.

For more information or to schedule a consultation, contact Chuck or Charles by calling toll free 1-888-PHONLPC or 1-888-746-6572.

Charles E. Lewis, Sr. and Charles E. Lewis, Jr.,
co-founders of Lewis Personal Consultants.

ORDER FORM

Name_____

Address_____

City/State/Zip_____

Tel. (optional)_____

Book	Qty.	Price	Total
Getting What You Want And Being Liked For It!		$19.95	

	Subtotal	_____
California residents add 8.25% sales tax		_____
Shipping & Handing		$4.25
Total		_____

Payment: Check   Money Order
              Visa   Mastercard   AMEX

Card #:_____

Name on card:_____

Signature:_____

Exp. Date:_____

Make check or money order payable to :
Littlejohn Publishing

Send to:
Littlejohn Publishing
9903 Santa Monica Blvd., Suite 627
Beverly Hills, CA. 90212

Please allow 3 to 4 weeks for delivery

If you are not satisfied with your purchase, simply return it
within 30 days and receive a full refund of your purchase price.
No questions asked.